PROSPERITY

IN THE AGE OF

DECLINE

How to Lead Your Business and Preserve Wealth through the Coming Business Cycles

BRIAN BEAULIEU AND ALAN BEAULIEU

WILEY

For general information about our other products and services, please contact our Customer
Care Department within the United States at (800) 762-2974, outside the United States at
(317) 572-3993 or fax (317) 572-4002.

Wiley publishes in a variety of print and electronic formats and by print-on-demand. Some
material included with standard print versions of this book may not be included in e-books or
in print-on-demand. If this book refers to media such as a CD or DVD that is not included in
the version you purchased, you may download this material at http://booksupport.wiley.com.
For more information about Wiley products, visit www.wiley.com.

ISBN 978-1-118-80989-1 (cloth); ISBN 978-1-118-93320-6 (ebk);
ISBN 978-1-118-93321-3 (ebk)

Printed in the United States of America

10 9 8 7 6 5 4 3 2 1

CONTENTS

1 Results That No One Can Ignore

You *Can* Successfully Prepare for an Unknown Future

You and I must make tough decisions with imperfect knowledge. That is what business leaders and investors do every day. The world is an uncertain place, and according to many people, it is an unknowable future. Yet paradoxically, most of us at times assume that current trends, be they financial, cultural, or political, will last into the future. This latter assumption presupposes that we can see the future. It is into the vortex of trends, uncertainties, and risk that we all plunge daily.

You address major decisions regularly. Sixty-five percent of businesses in America employ more than 100 people. We chose the word *people* and this approach over a discussion on labor as a factor of production because the latter is more sterile and would eliminate the often gut-wrenching nature of the decisions you make. Talking about people emphasizes the importance of those decisions and the risk involved in making the wrong decision. The decisions you make will have a direct impact on people's lives.

You are also likely directly or indirectly responsible for the decision making involved in the $875.1 billion in nondefense capital goods shipments made last year or the $117.8 billion in capital goods shipments related to the defense industry. Should you make the

1

capital commitment that could potentially make or break the future of the company?

All decisions involve risk to the health of the firm, to the financial well-being of people who are depending on you, and to your personal wealth and well-being. This book is about how you can minimize the uncertainties and thus minimize the risk in decision making and prosper. We show you that you can have 94.7 percent confidence in what the economy will be doing and that you can prosper professionally and personally with that knowledge through both the short and the longer term.

You are also no doubt an investor to one degree or another and have an interest in the $18.7 trillion U.S. stock market. The decisions you make here are extremely important to your future success and wealth. Later in the book we present investment ideas that are age specific and driven by a solid, reasoned view of the economic future of the United States and its major trading partners. The world will face some significant difficulties, but you and your family can be financially successful.

We argue that common perceptions can result in misallocation of resources and unnecessary worry. People were obsessed with China supposedly stealing all of our manufacturing jobs and in the process growing to be the largest economic country in the world. Neither proved to be true. Some people did indeed make money on this assumption in the past, but clinging to this assumption can lead to expensive capital expenditure or personal investment mistakes. The current reality is that manufacturing as a percent of gross domestic product (GDP) is on the rise in the United States. The China-manufacturing fixed-trend assumption makes it nearly impossible to get an accurate view of the future. How can anyone put together a three- or five-year plan for company growth, or a winning investment strategy, with a false view of the future?

Low interest rates, burgeoning government debt, and an aging population are but three of the major driving trends we present in this book. We discuss which trends we think will last and what individual investors and business leaders should do with this knowledge. Understanding and acting upon these trends are the keys to prosperity in what will likely be an age of global economic decline.

Where Not to Look

Arguably half the battle in successfully gauging the future and prospering in that future comes from not being misled by false signals. Don't waste time analyzing data that aren't relevant or statistically useful. We think it helps to learn where and what not to look at before committing yourself to looking for answers and insight in the right places.

Confidence Indicators

People often use business and consumer confidence indicators as a means of determining the next bend in the economic road. Most of these just do not work well, as you will see in Table 1.1. There are other leading indicators that work very well; we will also discuss those.

Table 1.1   Confidence Indicators to Retail Sales

Series	Correlation	Months
Small Business General Business Conditions Index	0.11	n/a
University of Michigan Consumer Expectations Index—Monthly	0.11	10
Small Business Sales Expectations Index	0.28	2
University of Michigan Consumer Expectations Index—Rate-of-Change	0.28	7
Conference Board Consumer Confidence Index	0.50	4
Small Business Optimism Index	0.58	11

Popular confidence indicators include the:

- Conference Board Consumer Confidence Index
- University of Michigan Consumer Expectations Index
- Small Business Sales Expectations Index
- Small Business General Business Conditions Index
- Small Business Optimism Index

A quick word of explanation is in order regarding Table 1.1. Unless it is specifically stated otherwise, we used rate-of-change methodology for the comparisons. This allows for a smoothing of trend lines and thus an easier discernment of correlation and business cycle pressures. We have attached Appendix A with more information on the determination of rate-of-change and its value in forecasting.

We also show a correlation number. In case it has been a while since you were in school, this is a measure of the association between two variables. A coefficient of 1 means that there is a perfect positive correlation; thus, a change in one series predicts a change in the other series. A coefficient of 0 means the relationship is random. You therefore look for numbers that are closest to $+1$ or -1 as they will more accurately tell you of a forthcoming cyclical change in the second series. Generally, the closer the correlation coefficient is to 1, the better the results are. High correlations are not foolproof, but they are indicative of tools we can use to anticipate change. Correlations of less than 0.5 are not helpful as they will be wrong as often as they are right in seeing the next turn in the economy, your market, or your company. Pay close attention to this column when deciding if your currently used confidence indicator is worth the effort.

Note that the correlation coefficients are only a tool. We at ITR Economics apply our experience to the process. Two series may seem to have a low correlation coefficient, but it is our job to see whether that is caused by volatility, random spikes, or some unique circumstances in one of the data series (for instance, a company made an acquisition). However, although the correlation coefficients are subject to interpretation, they will serve our purpose of determining how generally useful each of the confidence indicators is in predicting changes in both retail sales (retail sales drive 67 percent of our economy) and U.S. total industrial production (our benchmark of the U.S. economy in general).

The column marked *months* is the median timing relationship between a high or a low in the hoped-for leading indicator and the subsequent high or low in the second series. You will note the "n/a" in the months column, as the correlation coefficient results show that the data results were meaningless. It is important to note that a lead time of four months or less is still helpful when we are dealing with rates-of-change, but it is best to think of four months or less as confirming input. The change in the direction in the economy is virtually upon you by the time there is confidence that the leading indicator has indeed changed direction versus simply looking at statistical noise. Ideally a lead time of seven months or more will give a business leader time to implement plans for either increased or decreased levels of activity.

In Table 1.1, we have ranked the various confidence indicators from the lowest correlations to the highest using the data commonly reported in print and other media. We think you will be surprised by how some of these well-thought-of indicators actually perform.

You probably noticed a popular indicator on that list—the University of Michigan's Consumer Expectations Index. This number is produced monthly and followed religiously by the media and many business leaders. As you can see in Table 1.1, the monthly data that are published and followed by many have a very low correlation to retail sales rate of change (0.11), rendering them just about useless. Figure 1.1 shows you how this much-followed monthly trend compares to the retail sales monthly data trend. As you can see, the index will not help retailers, wholesale distributors, or manufacturers anticipate consumer activity.

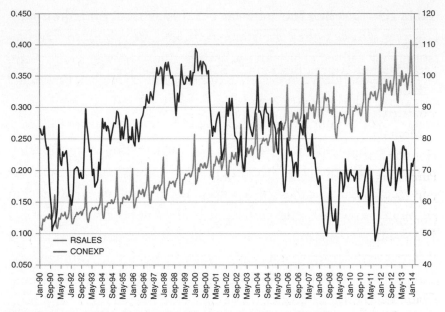

Figure 1.1 Retail Sales (Excluding Auto) to the University of Michigan's CEI

Table 1.2 examines the results of the monthly confidence index numbers and U.S. Total Industrial Production instead of retail sales (retails sales was used in Table 1.1). The Conference Board Consumer Confidence Index has the highest correlation at 0.85, which is impressive. Unfortunately, it leads turns in the overall economy by only a short four months. The Small Business Optimism Index has a helpful

Table 1.2   Confidence Indicators to U.S. Industrial Production

Series	Correlation	Months
Small Business General Business Conditions Index	0.13	n/a
Small Business Sales Expectations Index	0.25	3
University of Michigan Consumer Expectations Index	0.56	10
Small Business Optimism Index	0.70	6
Conference Board Consumer Confidence Index	0.85	4

Table 1.3 Leading Indicators to U.S. Industrial Production

Series	Correlation	Months
Small Business General Business Conditions Index	0.13	n/a
Conference Board U.S. Leading Indicator— Monthly	0.11	−8
Housing Starts	0.62	8
Purchasing Managers Index—Monthly	0.81	9
ITR Leading Indicator—Monthly	0.83	11
Conference Board U.S. Leading Indicators 1/12 Rate of Change	0.90	4

relationship with the economy, but there is still room for error at 0.70. That makes it useful, but you would not want to depend on it as a prominent forecasting tool, at least not without corroborating input from other leading indicators.

There are other popular leading indicators that are not related to business confidence. Some of these work exceptionally well, and we are happy to introduce them to you. However, while most of the indicators shown in Table 1.3 are popular they do not all work well.

We are proud to say that the ITR Leading Indicator is the best leading indicator based on correlation and lead time. This proprietary indicator is used heavily in our forecasting efforts.

The most consistently reliable results are achieved by using a *group* of leading indicators. Businesses that are positively correlated to the economy can use the ITR Leading Indicator, the Purchasing Managers Index from the Institute for Supply Management, and the Conference Board U.S. Leading Indicator to get a clear look around the next economic corner. None of these relies on business or consumer confidence as sole determinants of what will be, but rather they each use a number of empirical data points.

Table 1.4   Leading Indicators to Europe's Industrial Production

Series	Correlation	Months
Europe Leading Indicator	0.62	11
Europe Export Volume	0.75	−3
Europe Economic Sentiment Index	0.87	3

We have seen that confidence indicators do not work well in the United States. However, they work better in Europe, as the correlation coefficients in Table 1.4 demonstrate. The major drawback is the brevity of the lead time. The best indicator, the Europe Economic Sentiment Index, leads the Europe Industrial Production Index through highs and lows by only three months. It will often take longer than three months to confirm that a trend shift in the indicator has actually occurred. The economy may have changed direction by the time you know the indicator has a confirmed change in direction.

Politics

There is no help in looking to one political party over the other in determining whether the economy is going to be expanding or contracting. A look at the economic history of the United States shows that the economy expands under Republicans and Democrats in equal measure. Sorry, but there is statistically no difference.

It is also popular to believe that the economy is going to expand because it is a presidential election year. Since the inception of the Federal Reserve Board, the economy has been in recession 25 percent of the time, or 25 out of the last 100 years. Presidential election years have been recessionary 34.7 percent of the time based on our studies at ITR Economics. Investors and business leaders should not expect any extra help from the economy just because there is a presidential election.

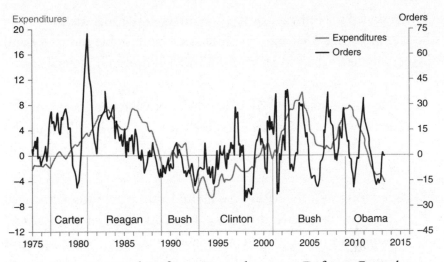

Figure 1.2 National Defense Expenditures to Defense Capital Goods N.O.

There is another popular myth in America that Republicans are good for defense spending and Democrats cut defense appropriations. The president is generally seen as the standard bearer for the party. A Republican in the White House is viewed as good news for the defense industry, and the opposite is true when a Democrat is residing at 1600 Pennsylvania Avenue. This has not been the case in modern times, as Figure 1.2 shows. Yet people will make predictions on the defense industry based on this false assumption. In doing so they may easily find themselves out of position to take maximum advantage of increased spending, or they may find themselves with too much labor and too little cash when the downturn comes.

Federal Reserve Board (The U.S. Version of Central Banks in Other Countries)

The Federal Reserve System, often known simply as *the Fed* or sometimes by the name of the governing body, the Federal Reserve Board (FRB), was created in December 1913, when President Woodrow

Wilson signed the Federal Reserve Act into law. The goal was to provide the nation with a safer, more flexible, and more stable monetary and financial system. The Fed's responsibilities fall into four general areas:

1. Influencing money and credit conditions through monetary policy, effectively done by influencing interest rates and by adjusting the money supply. The overarching goal is to pursue full employment and stable prices.

2. Supervising and regulating banks and other important financial institutions to ensure the safety and soundness of the nation's banking and financial system and to protect the credit rights of consumers.

3. Maintaining stability in the financial system and containing any systemic risk that may arise in financial markets.

4. Providing certain financial services to the U.S. government, U.S. financial institutions, and foreign official institutions and playing a major role in operating and overseeing the nation's payment systems.

These are, of course, important goals in terms of our national economic health and the well-being of individuals. A growing economy creates jobs, but an economy growing too fast can cause inflation or create an asset bubble, such as what we saw in home prices from 2000 to 2007. The Fed therefore strives to keep the economy growing at just the right speed and, if possible, avoid recessions as recessions involve layoffs, the antithesis of job growth.

People, including business leaders and politicians, believe in the Fed's ability to manage the economy. They put a lot of faith in that management and assume that they know when to act and what to do. Reality shows that the Fed has not been particularly good at maintaining a semi-constant growth rate, avoiding recessions, and providing for full employment.

There have been 18 recessions in the 100 years since the Federal Reserve System became law. Those 18 recessions have resulted in a total of 25 years of decline in industrial production in the United States. (Industrial production is our preferred benchmark for economic activity.) That is 18 times that the Fed either caused a recession to end an inflationary trend that it was charged to prevent in the first place or did not see the downturn coming and failed to act in time. There is a third possibility, and that is that the economy is too large to be controlled despite the enormous power the central bank wields.

Recessions are obviously tough on employment. The last three recessions alone resulted in the loss of 12,732,000 jobs in the private sector. The Fed could not prevent it because its power and abilities are limited in the face of the free-market economy. It is not that it is not competent or that it needs new superpowers; it is a function of complexity and the amazing strength of the free-market system. Any economy that is even somewhat market-driven will experience expansions and contractions. They have been occurring in economies around the world long before the Fed and other central banks were created.

The stated goal of the Fed is to provide stability to the banking system and financial markets. It is reasonable to ask what happened, then, in 2007 and 2008. Where was the Fed? The reality is that it did not see the Great Recession coming, and therefore it failed in its mandate to maintain the soundness of the banking and financial markets.

The end of this megatrend of the 2000s was foreseeable. In July 2007, ITR Economics warned readers through the *ITR Trends Report*™ to head for the exit because stock prices were about to shift into a declining trend. The long slide began a little longer than two months later. Proper preparation saved clients from losing millions of dollars and from lots of sleepless nights.

Please observe the comments and observations of Dr. Bernanke, chair of the Federal Reserve Board, during different stages of his tenure.

You may be among the millions of homeowners who enjoyed the aggressive run-up in home prices after the late 2001 price trough that accompanied the 2001–2002 recession. Many Americans believed a new reality was upon us and that the housing boom was set to continue indefinitely. Dr. Bernanke thought so, too, for in *February 2006* he stated, "Housing markets are cooling a bit. Our expectation is that the decline in activity or the slowing in activity will be moderate, that house prices will probably continue to rise." Housing prices peaked in June 2006.

In May 2007 Dr. Bernanke said:

> All that said, given the fundamental factors in place that should support the demand for housing, we believe the effect of the troubles in the subprime sector on the broader housing market will likely be limited, and we do not expect significant spillovers from the subprime market to the rest of the economy or to the financial system. The vast majority of mortgages, including even subprime mortgages, continue to perform well. Past gains in house prices have left most homeowners with significant amounts of home equity, and growth in jobs and incomes should help keep the financial obligations of most households manageable.[1]

You may remember that housing prices began to slide in October 2006 and continued to generally move lower through March 2011.

It was possible to see the upside in housing and foresee the downside. Early in the rising trend, we encouraged our clients to buy more real estate given the good rise ahead.[2] Housing prices rose in 2003,

---

[1]"The Subprime Mortgage Market" (speech, Federal Reserve Bank of Chicago's 43rd Annual Conference on Bank Structure and Competition, Chicago, IL, May 17, 2007).
[2]ITR Economics. *ITR Trends Report,* January 2003, Executive Summary page 1 and analysis on subsequent pages.

2004, and 2005 by 3.4 percent, 13.8 percent, and 7.5 percent, respectively. By March 2006 we were concerned that our clients were going to get caught in a significant recession and that they should therefore build cash reserves instead of going deeper into debt. We warned that the recession would begin in 2008, extend through 2009, and would be worse than anything in the prior 25 years. The recession began in early 2008, and the trough came in a thin 2.3 percentage points below the 2006 forecast estimate.

In January 2008 Dr. Bernanke said, "The Federal Reserve is not currently forecasting a recession."[3] The downturn in the Industrial Production Index began in November 2007 on a monthly basis and March 2008 on a quarterly moving average basis. GDP peaked in the third quarter of 2008. Even when the recession appeared imminent, the FRB forecast was not reliable. It was in June 2008 at the Boston Federal Reserve's fifty-second annual economic conference that the chair said, "the risk that the economy has entered a substantial downturn appears to have diminished over the past month or so."[4]

The Fed and Congress have not stopped recessions or eliminated the inherent risk in the financial systems. They simply cannot because it is an impossible task. It is, therefore, unwise to look to them to provide ongoing stability or accurate forecasts. Two months before Fannie Mae and Freddie Mac collapsed and were nationalized, Dr. Bernanke said they would make it through the storm. He was either misleading the country in an effort to restore confidence or simply not seeing the near future. Either way, it raises the question of credibility and makes us ask why so many people look to the Fed for guidance for their future. The reality is that the Fed is either not particularly good at seeing and/or

---

[3]Associated Press, "Bernanke: Fed Ready to Cut Interest Rates Again: 'We Stand Ready to Take Substantive Additional Action,' Fed Chief Says," NBCNews .com, last modified January 10, 2008, www.nbcnews.com/id/22592939.
[4]Craig Torres and Scott Lanman, "Bernanke Says Risk of 'Substantial Downturn' Has Diminished," Bloomberg, June 9, 2008, www.bloomberg.com/apps/news? pid=newsarchive&sid=aH6u3wsqwMFM.

communicating trouble coming at us, nor is it particularly good at containing the risk in financial markets.

The complex financial system cannot be so easily controlled even if the forward view is accurate. We can state that with great certainty because of history. Previous legislative efforts in the United States, Europe, Canada, and elsewhere would have worked to prevent economic and market contractions if it were possible to legislate or regulate economic risk into oblivion, but prior efforts failed, as will future efforts. In the United States we have had 24 stock market corrections since 1913. Past legislative and central bank efforts should have prevented the financial crisis of 2008, yet they did not. Now we have a massive piece of banking and financial legislation commonly known as Dodd Frank. The Fed has also increased its scrutiny and reporting requirements within the banking and finance community, and people believe that this will keep the problems from happening again. Do not be misled; they will happen again. Banks and financial institutions will find new ways to deal with existing laws, and those new ways will introduce more risk into the system until the system breaks once again. No entity can protect us from the results of that risk taking because of the inventiveness and legal astuteness of the high-stakes game of Wall Street banking and investment firms. The system is fluid and central banks cannot anticipate all the creativity in the industry.

Richard Fisher, president of the Federal Reserve Bank of Dallas and a member of the important decision-making Federal Open Market Committee (FOMC) stated in 2012 that "at best, the economic forecasts and interest rate projections of the FOMC are ultimately pure guesses."[5] Furthermore, he said that "forecasts issued by the FOMC

---

[5] "Fed's Fisher: All FOMC Forecasts 'Are Guesses,'" *Real Time Economics* (blog), *Wall Street Journal,* Feb 3, 2012, http://blogs.wsj.com/economics/2012/02/03/feds-fisher-all-fomc-forecasts-are-guesses.

are tactical judgments of the moment, made within a broader strategic context." The latter part of this statement means that they may say things that are consistent with the policy they wish to implement. For instance, an inflation dove who wants to keep interest rates low will forecast a low rate of inflation into the future.

Newspapers and Media

Our biggest competitors as forecasters are the *Wall Street Journal*, the *London Financial Times*, and other respected business and financial publications because people think that what appears in print is verifiable, actionable truth; but it's not. Newspapers, even the most prestigious, are not in the business of providing accurate economic forecasts; they're in the business of selling newspapers.

Most print publications have a particular position, point of view, or slant that underlies their reporting of the information they provide. To varying degrees, the same holds true with other media outlets: magazines, journals, television, radio, the Internet, and blogs. Most have certain positions that they seek to advance.

In days gone by, those who reported the news were considered objective, and most folks felt confident that they were reliable. That's drastically changed. As the media has expanded, especially on cable and blogs, many outlets have become specialized and more partisan. Many are dedicated to promoting a particular position or point of view. Some are conservative, others liberal, while others fill all levels between. We don't say this to malign these folks in any way; it appears to be either a part of the accepted culture or perhaps a function of being human.

In addition, we now have media outlets that specialize in business and finance. And each has spawned pundits who can't wait to tell us their opinions on what tomorrow will bring. It can get confusing because these pundits constantly seem to be disagreeing and often publicly bicker. Many of these media personalities owe their careers more to the fact that they look good, are articulate, and are entertaining rather than to their forecasting accuracy.

ITR Economics Forecast Accuracy

Knowing where not to look is only half an answer. Investors and decision makers need to know where to look. Our firm, ITR Economics, has a stellar long-term accuracy rate. That is why our forecasts and analyses are integral to the strategic planning process in myriad companies across a wide range of industries. (Please go to www.itreconomics.com to see a partial list of our clients.) Companies of all sizes and types can depend on our solid, nonpartisan, objective forecasts. We do not have a political agenda or any other goal except to be right in our projections. Everything we do is done with the single goal of providing our clients with dependable, actionable forecasts.

Our long-term accuracy rate on macroeconomic trends since the 1980s is 94.7 percent.[6] That is how long we have been stewards of ITR. Table 1.5 and Table 1.6 show our accuracy rates for 2011 for the U.S. and other global markets. Notice the duration column. That is how long the forecast was in place before the end of 2011. For instance, the forecast for U.S. GDP, at $13.525 trillion, was put in place in June 2010,

---

[6]We measure the mean absolute percentage error (MAPE) of the 12-month moving average (MMA) or 12-month moving total (MMT), whatever is relevant, of the subject series. The results are adjusted for any data revision to the subject series since the time of the forecast origination. (For example, if the 12 MMA is upward revised by 10 units, we upward revise the forecast by 10 units to account for the data revision before calculating the accuracy rate.)

We line up all the forecast errors for a given length of time (say four quarters away from origination) and then average those percentage errors. The quoted accuracy rate is the inverse of the error rate. So 97 percent accurate four quarters out means there was a 3 percent average deviation from the forecast 12MMA/T and the actual 12MMA/T four quarters out for all series.

Table 1.5 ITR Economics Forecast Accuracy 2012—United States

	Duration	Forecast	Actual	
U.S. GDP	18	$13.525 trillion	$13.332	(−1.4%)
U.S. ind. prod.	11	93.1 (12MMA)	93.8	(0.8%)
EU ind. prod.	11	101.1 (12MMA)	101.2	(0.1%)
CA ind. prod.	21	96.0 (12MMA)	96.0	(0.0%)
Retail sales	18	$2.116 trillion	$2.106	(−0.5%)
Housing	17	579 Ths units	607	(4.8%)
Employment	20	$141.1 million	139.9	(−0.9%)
CPI	17	2.9% Index	3.2%	

Table 1.6 ITR Economics Forecast Accuracy 2011—Foreign

Country	Duration	Accuracy
Germany	12	98.0%
France	18	99.9%
Italy	18	99.9%
United Kingdom	18	99.9%
Spain	18	98.6%
China	17	96.7%
Japan	15	95.9%
Brazil	14	96.7%
EU Industries	14	94.1%

18 months before the end of 2011. We had a 98.6 percent accuracy rate 18 months in advance. This is important because other firms constantly update their forecasts. Their forecasts shift up or down throughout the year, leaving their clients wondering what the coming year will actually look like. Our clients had a firm hand on the end of 2011 before the year even began.

Table 1.7   ITR Economics Forecast Accuracy 2012—United States

	Duration	Forecast	Actuals	
U.S. GDP	12	$13.593 trillion	$13.648	(0.4%)
U.S. ind. prod.	31	97.2 (12MMA)	97.2	(0.0%)
EU ind. prod.	12	100.4 (12MMA)	98.8	(−1.6%)
CA ind. prod.	8	96.7 (12MMA)	96.7	(0.0%)
Retail sales	30	$2.186 trillion	$2.131	(−2.5%)
Housing	6	743 Ths units	780	(5.0%)
Employment	33	$143.9 million	142.5	(−1.0%)
CPI	9	2.8% Index	2.1%	

Table 1.7 and Table 1.8 present domestic and foreign accuracy for 2012. The U.S. GDP forecast was put in place in December 2011 for the coming year. The year deviated a slim 0.4 percent from what we had estimated a whole year before. Our forecast accuracy for the more than 600 industries spanning the globe had an accuracy of 94.7 percent 12 months out from the forecast date. That is an accuracy our clients can use to their distinct competitive advantage. It is vital to capital expenditure budgets, changes in the labor force, lease negotiations,

Table 1.8   ITR Economics Forecast Accuracy 2012—Foreign

	Duration	Forecast	Actuals	
UK ind. prod.	13	101.2 (12MMA)	99.0	(2.2%)
EU GDP	12	€2.922 trillion	€2.931	(0.3%)
EU ind. prod.	12	100.4 (12MMA)	98.8	(−1.6%)
China ind. prod.	7	472.5 (12MMA)	474.2	(−0.6%)
Mexico ind. prod.	7	121.0 (12MMA)	121.2	(−0.2%)
All industries	12		5.3%	

and fixed-cost contract negotiations. Accurate forecasts reduce the uncertainty that shrouds the decision-making process for busy business leaders.

Table 1.9 presents ITR Economics' domestic and foreign accuracy for 2013. US GDP came in 0.7% higher than we had projected 12 months before the end of 2013. US Total Industrial Production came in 0.3% below our expectation. The largest deviation, Housing, had a forecast duration of one year and a forecast deviation of −2.3%. While we were much more conservative in our outlook for housing in 2013 than other forecasting firms, we were still a bit too upbeat with actual results coming in 2.3% below our expectations pronounced 12 months ahead of time.

Table 1.9   ITR Economics Forecast Accuracy 2013

	Duration	Forecast	Actuals	
U.S. GDP	12	$15.818 trillion	$15.966	(0.7%)
U.S. ind. prod.	10	99.9 (12MMA)	99.6	(−0.3%)
EU ind. prod.	20	101.9 (12MMA)	100.6	(−1.3%)
CA ind. prod.	15	98.7 (12MMA)	97.8	(−0.8%)
China ind. prod.	9	522.6 (12MMA)	520.1	(−0.5%)
Housing	12	945 Ths units	923	(−2.3%)
Retail sales	18	$2.189 trillion	$2.200	(0.5%)
Employment	24	$144.3 million	143.9	(−0.3%)

2 The Status Quo Never Was

Seven Major Trends and Assumptions That Won't Last

After the recession of 2008–2009, business leaders, politicians, economists, and pundits of every sort were struggling to define what the "new norm" would be. People feel that their world has been turned upside down, that the life they once knew is no longer conceivable, and that there is a new, more dangerous future ahead. They may be right about the more dangerous future, but they are certainly wrong to think that somehow a unique major disruption to the status quo has befallen us. What has happened is that economic conditions have changed, which they always do. It is usually human perception and flawed memories that make the changes seem seismic. The actual changes themselves are much more gradual and almost always foreseeable. We argue that perceptions of China surpassing the United States and flawed memories of the one-time conventional wisdom how inflation would not give way to deflation are at work now and that they combine in a way that makes it nearly impossible to get an accurate read on the future. How can one project future events if the trends driving the outlook are waning, to be replaced by newer, more relevant trends?

The status quo for the early part of the twenty-first century has been shattered, but that status quo was starkly different from the 1990s, which were remarkably different than the 1980s, which was a decade nothing like the 1970s. We think it best to assume that the status quo is a short-term experiential phenomenon and that change is the only constant that can be relied upon. What is the new norm? It is the same as the old norm: things will be different in the future.

Unfortunately, we humans seem to be hardwired to straight-line forecast. The current condition, especially if it has become common knowledge for even a little while, is typically expected to last indefinitely into the future. This expectation occurs many times in the most innocuous ways. Ask someone what the weather will be like tomorrow after it has rained for two days in row. A bad day at work can lead an employee of many years to grumble that his or her place of employment is a terrible place to work despite years of relative happiness. These are daily occurrences that rarely warrant a second thought. Straight-line thinking also occurs on a larger scale when people believe that what they are experiencing is the status quo and that it will endure and therefore they make no plans for an alternative future. This lack of openness to a different future can have disastrous consequences on a company or on individual investors. Businesses and individuals need to be prepared for seismic shifts and learn which major trends are real and which are nothing more than relatively temporary noise.

We begin this chapter by looking at previous trends that people thought would continue indefinitely before moving on to current assumptions that right now are widely accepted and unshakeable. We finish with a look at major trends now in place that are not going to last. This last section will set the stage for actions that should be taken corporately and personally to prosper in an age of decline.

Unstoppable Trends That Suddenly Stopped

Population Growth Will Kill Humankind

Anyone educated in the 1970s will remember the mandatory reading regarding population growth and the limited ability of our planet to sustain life in the future, given the breakneck speed at which the world population was growing. That argument actually surfaced centuries ago, in 1798 to be specific, in a thesis put forth by Thomas Malthus.

Thomas Malthus's assumption was straightforward. Food production would not keep up with reproduction as the latter was geometrical and the former arithmetical. Writing in 1798, he posited that the British population could potentially grow to 121 million while food production could not possibly grow to support more than 77 million. By the end of the 1800s, 44 million would be theoretically doomed to starvation. War, disease, and poverty would ensue. His logic was seemingly sound. His population growth estimate was based on early actual population growth in the United States, which he used as the unfettered potential of humankind. He applied all the land possible and all the technology possible at the time to determine what food production would be like 100 years out.

His obvious mistake was straight-line thinking in terms of food production brought about by the assumption of stagnant agricultural technology. The 1800s saw the introduction of the McCormick reaper, John Deere and Leonard Andrus's steel plow, the practical grain drill, the first grain elevator, a practical mowing machine, irrigation, and commercial sale of mixed chemical fertilizers. All these advancements were unknown to the prognosticator of doom.

The value and impressiveness of human ingenuity has been demonstrated throughout history. Yet that has not stopped others from following after Thomas Malthus under the persistent assumption that human population growth would harm us all, largely because of food problems. Take for example *The Population Bomb* by Paul and Anne Ehrlich, written in 1971. The cover states, "Population Control or Race to Oblivion?" The premise was simple: mass starvation of humans as food and energy prices skyrocketed in response to massive demand and limited supply. They argued for strict population controls throughout the world, additives to the water supply to produce sterility in the population, and other draconian (and unnecessary) measures.

Anyone in school in the 1970s remembers this book and the ongoing fear of population growth.

The Population Bomb was followed in 1972 by *The Limits to Growth* by Donella Meadows, Dennis Meadows, Jørgen Randers, and William Behrens III. The book modernized Malthus's theories but ended by restating that population growth is exponential and the technological ability to expand resources is linear. They stressed that they are not writing doomsday scenarios like Malthus's, but two of their three scenarios result in a twenty-first century collapse. It has not happened, but anyone older than 50 probably remembers reading the book and "learning" the dangers of having too many children. The belief is with us today. There is no basis for it given humans' proven ability to adapt new materials and new technology, but it is not difficult to find people who still believe large families are harmful and that population control is necessary.

Individuals and businesses who bought into this thinking and assumed they were major life-changing trends would have invested their capital and energy in unprofitable areas if they bothered to invest at all. (Why bother to invest if the end of the world draws near?) Following this megatrend would keep an investor from buying land for housing developments, investing in commodity futures, or borrowing heavily in a pre-inflation environment. Opportunities would be missed and leaders would have taken their team in the wrong direction.

Cheap Oil Is Here to Stay

Readers older than 50 years of age will remember when oil prices were low and seemed destined to stay that way. Prices in the 1950s ranged from $2.60 to $3.10 per barrel. The next decade saw prices move in an even narrower band of $3.00 to $3.40 per barrel. Easy energy prices seemed likely to last forever and energy budgeting was easy. There was no reason to expect a dramatic change in the economic landscape or in oil prices. Prices edged up some from early 1970 to December 1973 when prices seemingly soared to $4.30. Still, the status quo seemed to be holding, and the major trend, cheap oil, seemed more than reasonable. One month later the price of a barrel of crude oil was $10.10. Prices trebled in the next seven years to end the decade at $32.50 per barrel.

Oil prices first started to rise in 1971 in response to a weaker U.S. dollar. Richard Nixon's decision to take the United States off the gold standard in 1971 resulted in a devaluation of the U.S. dollar. The Organization of Petroleum Exporting Countries (OPEC) responded to the Bretton Woods Accord by increasing the price of oil. Tensions were further increased because of the Yom Kippur War in October 1973. OPEC used oil as a weapon and soon declared an embargo against nations that supported Israel in the war, including the United States.

The rapid escalation in oil prices was a boon to oil-producing nations and a cause of energy-related inflation in the United States and other importing nations. The economy stagnated and inflation was fueled, leading to a period that came to be known as stagflation. OPEC nations prospered with Western dollars, and industrialized nations adjusted to a new reality. In addition, the United States and other nations turned to new energy-saving technology, such as fuel-efficient cars, and a new energy era began in the United States and around the world.

The initial change occurred quickly from December 1973 to January 1974, and then a slow decade of ever more painful inflation and stagnant growth passed. The status quo of the previous two decades was invalidated. Business leaders who were slow to change found themselves out of business as they were unable to manage higher energy prices successfully. This period was followed by forecasts in the late 1970s and in the early 1980s that oil would eventually reach $400 a barrel, and the Peak Oil Theory became dogma for a new status quo. As President Ford once said, "The pendulum had swung full circle."

The thought in the first half of the seventies was that cheap gas would last forever. Then fear took over and people thought oil and gas prices would never stop rising. Both views were wrong and led people to make tragic and costly mistakes in the futures market and in inventory management. We cannot predict when the next technology will come along that will greatly reduce the global demand for oil and thus bring prices down. We can tell you that demand for energy will keep increasing, and the upside pressure on oil prices will be the predominant theme until newer technologies replace fossil fuels. Natural gas will help but only as the demand for industrial, home, and power generation use increases from today's levels.

Japan Will Surpass the United States as the World's Economic Superpower

Japan's trade relationship with the United States began in the late 1800s. It was an ally to the United States in World War I, as we were to them in the Sino-Japanese War and Russo-Japanese War. Japan provided affordable goods to America in the Great Depression and served as an important export destination to hard-pressed U.S. firms in the 1930s. World War II obviously disrupted what had been a mutually beneficial relationship, albeit a relationship that favored the United States. The United States exported to Japan more than Japan sent to the United States. Japan's return to self-determination in 1952 following the war resulted in a mutually agreed-upon, export-oriented trade strategy that limited U.S. exports to Japan. The next 13 years saw Japan become an increasingly important trading partner. This may sound very similar to the early U.S. relationship with China, and indeed there are many similarities and lessons to learn from it.

The relationship was essentially amicable from 1952 to 1965 as the United States enjoyed many Japan-made consumer goods. Then a shift occurred. The balance of trade shifted in 1965 when imports into the United States from Japan reached $2.4 billion while U.S. exports to Japan stood at $2.1 billion. The best-selling Japanese imports were radios and television sets (remember transistors?). The trade imbalance would continue to grow over the next two decades.

Some Japanese companies, beginning with Sony in 1970, set up operations in the United States. American jobs were created and products were made here that U.S. consumers wanted to buy. Despite all that, fear began to grow. Americans began to fear that Japan would surpass the United States as an economic power through the use of amazing technology, impressive manufacturing techniques, and an ability to make what Americans wanted to buy.

Fear of Japan's strength and abilities grew in 1973 with the oil crisis. Fuel-efficient cars made by Toyota, Datsun (now Nissan), and Honda were in demand by an oil-thirsty country. General Motors, Ford, and Chrysler were a decade behind and it showed.

Trade confrontations began in the 1970s and would continue into the next decade. The situation became even tenser as Americans feared losing vital national security technology and canceled the purchase of U.S. manufacturer Fairchild Semiconductor by Fujitsu in 1987.

Troubles in the United States, particularly in heavy industry, led to layoffs and slower growth in key businesses. Japanese businesses were gaining ground in the United States as U.S. firms were showing the strain of years of inflation and arguably a failure to reinvest in new technologies, methodologies, and markets. America's fears increased when Japan became the second-largest foreign investor in the United States. Americans were concerned that Japan was buying America. Those fears were increased with Sony's acquisition of CBS Records and Columbia Pictures in 1988 and 1989, respectively.

The anti-Japan fear led to Japan bashing. The underlying supposition was that Japan was taking over and America was helpless to stop it. People were sure of it. The U.S. government fought the so-called takeover. Politicians railed against Japan's supposedly unfair advantages.

Businesses were worried about competing against this amazing techno-
logically driven nation. Strategies, court actions, and countless hours
were devoted to combating a future that never was. Japan's economic
bubble burst and the threat was gone. A decade or more of fear was over,
and the underlying assumptions were proven false. Ironically, we no
longer fear Japan; heck, people rarely even ask us about Japan anymore.
It no longer seems to matter that imports from Japan are more than
two times greater than exports to that nation, and the trade imbalance
is an impressive $73.8 billion. Japan's quick fade from the limelight did
not help the firms who built a future on the assumption of an unstop-
pable Japan. Foreign direct investment into Japan in the late 1980s
turned out to be a bad idea, and the economic might of Japan-made
products waned quickly in the face of the newest competitor in the
world—China. Firms too focused on Japan missed tremendous opportunities in the nearby giant.

Inflation

Younger readers may not know what life was like in the 1970s and therefore have no idea how to lead a business in a period of inflation. It has
been a generation since we have had systemic, long-term inflationary
pressures.

We have already discussed what was going on with U.S. fears relative to Japan. Beneath that fear was another reality that seemed to linger
as a permanent part of the economic landscape. That reality was called
inflation. It was a time of real, honest-to-goodness price escalation that
seemed to be a fabric of life and a part of doing business. Business leaders had to factor inflation into decisions involving everything, including
labor, purchasing, sales, long-term contracts, and accounting methods.
Inflation was part of the daily business environment, and the assumption was that it was going to stay. It became a global event.

The U.S. Consumer Price Index (CPI) in November 1965 registered inflation at a benign 1.6 percent. Four short years later the CPI

had risen to 6.2 percent, and it did not stop there. Developed nations saw an average inflation rate of 13 percent in 1974, and it remained in the 7 to 12 percent range for the next eight years. It may be hard to imagine that economies and businesses could function in that environment, but they did. The U.S. CPI hit a high-water mark of 11 percent in September 1981.

Federal Reserve Chairman Paul Volcker decided to get aggressive and tightened monetary policy to squeeze inflation out of the economy. He was eventually successful, but it took the significant economic downturn of the early 1980s to reign in the inflationary pressures. The CPI returned to 1.6 percent again in May 1986, 20 years after the upward spiral began.

Businesses built strategies and tactics around an inflation model. They did not have much choice, but nonetheless they succumbed to straight-line thinking and believed that inflation was the way of life. Pricing models, union negotiations, and management decisions were built on that assumption. The assumption of ongoing inflation led management to make union concessions regarding wages and pension benefits that would ultimately contribute to corporate bankruptcies, not the least of which was General Motors' famous bankruptcy in 2009. Federal, state, county, and local governments, and the nation as a whole, are still living under the threat of massive unfunded liabilities that have their roots in the untrue assumption that inflation was inevitable. The pension programs and the related liabilities were based on an inflation model that is long gone.

The Housing Bubble

Housing prices on new homes began to ascend in earnest off a July 2002 low of $175,600 (U.S. median). Money was cheap and mortgages were readily available thanks to the Community Reinvestment Act, the Federal Reserve Board, and the clever use of derivatives in the financial community. Mortgage-backed securities allowed bankers and mortgage companies to offer mortgages at amazing rates and under very favorable variable-rate terms. It seemed that the status quo of easy credit, higher home prices, and easy wealth creation for people was a winning formula that people could count on. Young and old believed this megatrend would provide for easy wealth creation and that it would last forever. Prices on new homes soared to a median of $250,800 by February 2006. Existing home prices shot up $69,900 from December 2001 to June 2006, creating a bubble in perceived personal wealth. It was a wonderful time, and most people, including Dr. Bernanke of the Federal Reserve, were not concerned about a housing and financial crash.

As mentioned in Chapter 1, in January 2003 we encouraged our clients to buy more real estate. We began warning our clients of the coming dangers in 2006 and encouraged them to build cash reserves and to make other preparations. ITR Economics warned that the recession would begin in 2008 and extend through 2009, and history shows that is what happened.

A belief in the housing bubble megatrend led to financial disaster for millions of financially stretched Americans and millions more as the recession led to massive layoffs. The signs of disaster were there, but first a person needed to believe that the status quo would not last in perpetuity.

The Stock Market

The S&P 500 began to rise off a February 2003 low, and money began to pour into the market. A megatrend was born and investors were enjoying what became a five-year boom that saw the market rise a total of 84.2 percent. Young people were planning to retire at 50, and older people were dreaming of truly golden years. Believing in this megatrend became expensive as the market headed for a crash that saw the market fall 52.6 percent between October 2007 and February 2009.

Retirement accounts, such as 401(k)s, were devastated, and would-be retirees had to work additional years to try to restore their nest eggs.

Today's Trends That Won't Last Forever

China

China has been in growth mode for decades. That certainly qualifies as a major trend, and in most people's minds it is a trend that is not about to end any time soon. A 2013 global survey of nearly 40,000 people by Pew Research determined that a majority of respondents expected China to overcome the United States as the world's top economy. Half of the Americans polled felt the same way. The Organization of Economic Cooperation and Development believes that China will overtake the United States in three years. That would mean that President Obama would be the last U.S. president to lead an economically supreme U.S. economy. Slightly more than a third of the Pew respondents already thought China was the largest economy.

In case you are wondering, America has been the world's leading economic power since 1871, and today it contributes 21.9 percent to the world's total gross domestic product (GDP) of $71.707 trillion, as compared with 11.5 percent from China. The United States has a GDP of about $15.7 trillion, and China's is in second place at about $8.24 trillion. A quick check will show you that China is about 52.5 percent of the size of the United States. It would seem that those folks who believe China is already larger than the United States have not had access to the facts!

Figure 2.1 illustrates how the largest slices of world GDP are distributed among the 15 largest economies. If you favor an economy but don't see it listed separately in the pie chart stemming from IMF data, it is because it falls under the category of "Other." "Others" rise into the top 15 through time just as some of the top 15 of today will slip into the anonymity of "Other" someday.

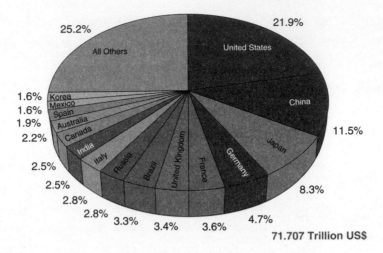

Figure 2.1   World GDP, Current Prices (Billions of U.S. Dollars)
Source: IMF.

It is not likely that China will surpass the United States. We realize that may appear to be a bold statement to make, but logic and an
understanding of trends are on our side. Here are six reasons why China
will not surpass the United States in economic might.

1. Only half of the Pew respondents had a favorable view of China,
   but a much larger segment saw the United States as a partner. That
   is an important consideration when it comes to treaties, long-term
   relationships upon which business relationships are built, and the
   trust that exists between allied nations (as in the United States
   and the United Kingdom). A favorable view by others enhances
   long-term global relationships and stability. It is unlikely that
   China will gather the global goodwill needed to become the global
   leader of the developed world.

2. Only 37 percent of America has a favorable view of China. It was
   51 percent two years ago. The declining favorable view could make
   it more difficult for China to sell big-ticket items into the United
   States, such as automobiles or Chinese-branded computers, to
   name two large potential markets. An anti-China sentiment could

quickly cause a backlash resulting in declining Chinese exports into the United States and a corresponding loss of economic growth and decline in job creation.

3. China's pollution will be hard to clean up. It has the worst smog in the world, and the amount of carbon dioxide emissions is getting worse, not better. Decades of poor environmental manufacturing practices have rendered about 40 percent of China's river water unfit for human consumption. These problems will take years to clean up at a cost of trillions of dollars. Becoming a mature, equal partner on the global scene will erode China's competitive position in the world export market.

4. China is committed to growing a middle class to compensate for the future reduction in exports. That is a good plan but a difficult one. The growth of a middle class means ongoing wage increases, which by their very nature will increase the cost of goods produced and further reduce global competitiveness. Additionally, China's demographic trends do not support a favorable outcome consistent with its middle-class ambition.

5. China has a growing income inequality problem, which could quickly lead to serious social problems and instability in the country. Beijing has been dealing with the problem through social spending, which requires tax increases on income producers. This transfer of wealth benefits the have-nots but also increases the cost of goods and services within the nation and in the global export environment.

6. Lastly, China's one-child policy with unofficial gender selection has produced a demographic imbalance that will be tough to fix. A fertility rate of 1.6 will make it hard to produce future taxpayers who will support an aging population. The solutions are to export the elderly, reduce their standard of living as they retire, or increase taxes to support the older generation. The latter course seems the most likely to us.

Decades of living on steroids has left this tiger economy with serious problems that strongly suggest that the status quo trend that is China should not be extended into the future by those peering beyond tomorrow. The status quo will not last, and apparently a significant portion of the world's economy will be surprised that this current major trend did not last. Business leaders who are slow to adapt to a changing China will lose significant capital and potentially find themselves trying to export increasingly expensive goods to the rest of the world. Near-sourcing is a new and very real trend that is going to disrupt the status quo that many people seem to think is inevitable. Businesses that embrace the new reality will have a natural price hedge as well as a buffer against potential internal social strife within China and other parts of Asia.

Stimulus Spending Is Needed and Helpful

Stimulus spending is in vogue around much of the world and has certainly become a major trend since 2008. It has also become the status quo in that most nations have been engaging in stimulus spending of one kind or another for five years. Most people believe that it is a worthwhile use of funds, whether the money is freshly created, borrowed, or extracted out of the economy through taxation before being reinjected to suit the government's concepts of economic fairness and right and wrong. There is good reason to believe that once again the majority may have succumbed to false assumptions.

Three economist researchers, one each from the St. Louis Federal Reserve, the University of California economics department, and the Bank of Canada, looked at stimulus spending in the United States and in Canada to see if government deficit spending in times of high unemployment produced a positive multiplier effect and thus boosted economic activity. A multiplier of 1 means that $1 of government spending generates $1 of economic activity. They studied data in the United States from 1890 to 2010 and 1921 to 2011 in Canada. High unemployment was defined as more than 6.5 percent in the United States and 7 percent in Canada.

The researchers found that deficit-financed stimulus spending produced positive results in Canada. The multiplier reached 1.6 during periods of high unemployment as compared to 0.44 during periods when unemployment was below 7 percent. The same did not hold true in the United States, where the multiplier was below 1 at all levels of unemployment. The government borrowed $1 to stimulate the economy and generated about 64 cents of economic activity when unemployment was high and about 78 cents when unemployment was below the 6.5 percent threshold. The borrowed dollar must be repaid, with interest, in what is a losing proposition for taxpayers.

Will These Trends Endure?

- A strong U.S. dollar
- Investment in U.S. government bonds as your primary retirement vehicle
- Low interest rates
- Negligible inflationary pressures
- The aging population
- Mounting public debt
- Sentiment that the end is near for the United States

These trends will not last indefinitely. But *some* will last for most of the next two decades, and others are about to change. That is precisely the problem when trying to define the future. We will discuss which trends we think will last and what individuals and business leaders should do with this knowledge. Understanding and acting upon these trends are the keys to prosperity in what will likely be an age of global economic decline.

3 Preparing for Prosperity—Good News for 2015 and 2016

Do You Have Enough?

The year 2014 is a year of midterm elections, which will invariably result in myriad loud and argumentative interpretations about where the U.S. economy currently is and where it is going. The first order of business is to ignore the rhetoric. Just tune it out. Instead, pay attention to the key leading indicators we presented in Chapter 1.

We are expecting the economy's rate of growth to slow noticeably in the second half of 2014. Retailers will be complaining about lackluster Christmas sales, and job growth will be ho-hum at best. Avoid the human tendency to straight line what we expect will be lackluster economic news into the indefinite future. The sluggishness in consumer spending and in business-to-business activity should end in the second quarter of 2015. How will you know things are going to pick up in the second half of 2015? Easy: look at the following leading indicators.

It is important to find out whether you lead, lag, or are coincident to the macro environment and to determine your timing relationship to the ITR Leading Indicator and other key indicators. Knowing the timing relationship is key to the planning and implementation process. You can visit www.itreconomics.com to learn more; for our discussion here, we will assume you run essentially coincident with the general economic environment. This means you turn up and down in line with broad economic measures such as Gross Domestic Product (GDP), U.S. industrial production, and retail sales.

The ITR Leading Indicator should be in a clear rising trend by late 2014 or early 2015. We put this one first because it is designed to be one of the earliest leading indicators to signal a change in the direction of the economy. A fourth-quarter-2014 low in our leading indicator means you will be busier in the second half of 2015.

As we've stated before, it is dangerous to rely on a single indicator. Instead, look for improvement in the following indicators to confirm the pending improvement in the economy and in your business:

- Corporate bond prices
- Conference Board's U.S. Leading Economic Index
- Institute for Supply Management's Purchasing Managers Index
- Housing starts

Chapter 8 provides a lot information and detail about where these indicators come from and how best to use them. For now, just know that there will be reasonably clear signals that the economy and your business will be heating up. You can take these positive signals as proof that it is time to start implementing plans for higher levels of activity. Note that we said *implementing*—because the time to do the planning is beforehand. The leading indicators are a call to action to take the plan down from the shelf and *put it into action*.

Again, Chapter 8 presents a longer, more in-depth discussion of what to do in various phases of the business cycle. For now, ask yourself if you have enough of the factors of production to handle more customers, data, material, leads, and employees in a way that will keep you profitable. This requires you and your management team to *honestly assess* your current capabilities. Ask yourselves: Where are the bottlenecks? Who or what might block expansion? What investments do I need to make now to ensure I can grow with the economy?

Although the answers to these questions will vary from one organization to another, the concept of immediate action will remain constant. Spend the time and the money to get ready for a brighter future despite the ambiguity evident in the press—and the minds of people around you.

During 2014, the economic sluggishness described earlier and the uncertainty that generally accompanies it will likely be clearly evident in the stock market. Be ready to invest in equities in the first half of 2015. There is no sense in trying to time the absolute low point in the turn; just gather up your cash and plunge back in when it seems fairly certain the market is back into a sustainable upswing. The words *fairly certain* are key. You will have to assume some risk if the goal is to maximize return on the funds invested. Waiting until everyone is sure there is a bull market underway will produce noticeably more tepid results.

What Will 2015, 2016, and 2017 Look Like?

Our GDP forecast (adjusted for inflation) for the United States is shown in Figure 3.1.

We can see that these will be years of solid growth, with the following growth rates forecasted:

2015: 2.6 percent

2016: 3.3 percent

2017: 3.7 percent

Consumer activity should be healthy, both in real and nominal dollar terms (unadjusted and adjusted for inflation). This will provide

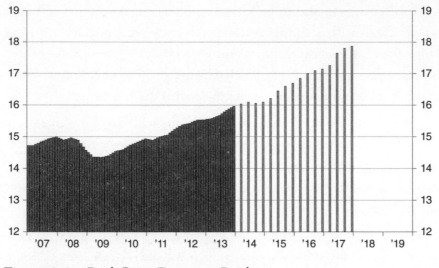

Figure 3.1   Real Gross Domestic Product

increased demand for manufacturers and thus also benefit the whole-salers and distributors throughout much of the economy. Freight companies, airlines, hotels, theme parks, and tourism in its many forms should all do well. Investors will enjoy solid gains in equities, unemployment will go down, and the prosperity will form a positive upward spiral.

The medical industry will also benefit from the burgeoning retirement population and the natural expansion in the economy in general. More customers on Medicare and on other insurance will stimulate a period of growth for businesses and investors in this sector.

State and local governments are already seeing some improvement in tax receipts. They'll likely be enjoying additional increased revenues in this period because the general economy will be growing. Although the unfunded pension liability issues will be far from settled, expect more spending on construction, services, and normal government procurement in 2015, 2016, and 2017 as government goes about the business of satisfying its constituents. Building contractors will find more bidding opportunities and a return to healthier margins.

Many factors—ranging from pavers having more to do, to upgraded information technology equipment—will be in play. But keep in mind that the good times in this sector are likely to never be as good as they were in the halcyon days of unfettered federal and local government expansion when the reality of retiring baby boomers was not on the proverbial doorstep.

We urge you to look at leading indicators because they are objective and not subject to nearly as much spin or interpretation as the spoken word. In terms of the written word, you will probably see chatter about how consumers seem to be doing their job vis-à-vis the economy by being out there and spending money. It will come down to whether they are spending freely enough. The United States generally needs retail sales, adjusted for inflation, to grow at a 2.5 percent year-over-year pace or better for the overall economy to see some lift. That pace of retail sales growth generally means that the consumer is in good financial shape and has a desire to spend. According to the Federal Reserve, household debt in 2013 was the lowest it's been in 29 years. Balance sheets have been repaired for the vast majority of Americans, at least for now. And if the Americans are spending money, the world has an extremely important consumer market available to it. U.S. home prices will be a crucial part of ensuring this ability to spend money is present. A leveling off—or a slower version of the rising trend—in the 2013 home prices would be very healthy in terms of setting the table for a good economic run in 2015–2017, as this would have a positive effect on housing affordability.

Of course, other factors will affect whether consumers have the means and ability to spend money. Not limited to the United States is the question of higher taxes—and how deep into the consumer's discretionary income pocket central governments will thrust their hands. It seems probable now that government is going to be digging deeper and deeper into our pockets as it strives to cover its debt and the requirements of an aging population. Aggressive or loose monetary policy can help in this arena for a while. Maintaining very low interest rates, growing the money supply, and not putting too much pressure on banking systems to narrow their scope of profitability will combine to help offset government fiscal policies. We are assuming in our forecast of general rise 2015–2017 that the central bankers of the world will remain far more concerned about deflation and a return to recession than about future inflation. If the central bankers become serious about inflation sooner than 2017–2018, it could mitigate the economy's ability to grow during this period.

We are implicitly assuming that a lot of the consternation the midterm elections and the implementation of the Affordable Care Act (aka Obamacare) brought about will be settled within the United States as we head through 2015. Although the U.S. Congressional Budget Office is forecasting that Obamacare will eventually lead to the loss of 2.3 million jobs in the United States, most of this loss occurs after 2016—and will continue over an extended period. And it is only a loss in that new jobs won't be created, as opposed to current jobs being done away with. A higher minimum wage law in the United States may have the same effect, although statistics are there to argue whether this is true. The most important thing is that people get used to their circumstances, adjust, and *always* find a way to get back to the business of consuming.

We suspect that consumerism will be the initial engine of renewed growth in 2015 in the United States, and that will spark consumerism and exports in economies across the globe. Business cycle rise is not always at the purview of the consumer. We have had numerous business cycles in the United States and in other economies where the initial impetus for business cycle rise came from business-to-business activity—as we see in Figure 3.2.

It doesn't seem that business-to-business activity will be the most probable source of the business cycle upturn in 2015—because we don't expect that there will be much of a falling off in business-to-business

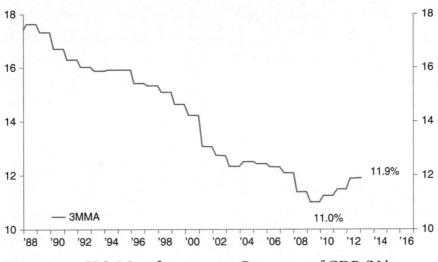

Figure 3.2 U.S. Manufacturing as a Percentage of GDP (Value Added)

activity during 2014 and early 2015. That is one of the reasons why 2014 looks like a soft landing; business-to-business is not likely to go into a slump. The increase in manufacturing in the United States and Mexico measured as share of GDP supports this view. Insourcing, or onshoring, is a very real trend—and one destined to provide a floor to the business cycle in 2014 and added lift in 2015 and beyond. However, it will not be the largest swing variable as we move out of 2014 and into 2015. Keep in mind that retail sales account for about 67 percent of GDP in the United States.

It is imperative that business leaders aggressively take advantage of this rising trend. Assemble your marketing plans, work on your customer relationships, make sure your supply chain can handle the increased load, look for global opportunities—and enjoy the rise.

4 Depression Driver

Demographics

There are demographic trends that mean eventual significant financial distress for the United States. These trends are dominant. We are aging as a nation. We have entitlement programs tied to aging that are not financially viable. We will go broke and experience the Great Depression of the 2030s unless something changes.

We need to change either the demographic trends themselves or how we fund caring for our elderly. Both of these will be extremely difficult to do. We are assuming in our projection of a coming Great Depression that what is difficult to change will not be altered and that the path of least resistance will be adhered to when it comes to demographics. The result of following this path of least resistance (what we think of as political inertia) will be broad-based financial distress, which will be an important contributing factor to the Great Depression of the 2030s.

Demographic trends are driven by birth rates, mortality rates, and immigration. Significant assumptions need to be made when projecting demographic trends, and some folks are quick to point out that such forecasts are never right. For our purposes, they do not need to be right, just generally true. It doesn't matter if the population projections are off by 10 million or more when you are talking about a total U.S. population of approximately 400 to 438 million by the year 2050.

The trend is there whether you are talking about 400 million people or 438 million people. It is the *trend* that is significant to our work as is the trend's current starting point of 312 million people in the United States as of mid-2013. Any way you slice it, there will be a lot more people living in this country in a relatively short period. If it were only a matter of a lot more people being a part of the economy, the consequences would not necessarily point in the direction of a financially difficult period. It is the number of *aging* people and how we deal with that reality that will be the impetus for the financial stress.

Before getting into details, let's take a moment to acknowledge that black swan events could seriously alter the demographic landscape, for better or for worse. A malady could arise that would significantly reduce the number of older people in the United States and thus alleviate the financial distress. Military action, a substantial change in rational immigration laws, or some *force majeure* could rob us of an appreciable portion of the younger generation(s) that would otherwise be available to us in the future. By definition, there is no point assigning probabilities to any one of these events. However, note that barring some trend-altering significant black swan event, the trends we are going to look at portend a need for change if we are going to avoid economic distress.

Keep in mind that although we are, indeed, facing a significant issue vis-à-vis the aging population, the United States is relatively well positioned in this regard compared with our major trading partners. We demonstrate this at the end of this chapter; this relatively superior position regarding demographics plays very well into our prognosis that the U.S. economy will remain the preeminent economy on this planet for generations to come. Demographics, ingenuity, and economic prowess are powerful forces that will enable the United States to be an economic leader for a long time. However, political inertia is likely to mean that we aren't going to be able to avoid the relatively near-term negative effects of our aging population.

More People, More Older People

We are not only becoming more numerous, but we are also becoming older as a people. This reality must be balanced with the likelihood that there are going to be more and more people of all ages living in the United States in the years ahead. It is far too easy to draw wrong conclusions about our aging dilemma and the fate of the United States if we forget that we are growing in total numbers. Table 4.1 uses U.S. Census Bureau data to show just how many more people there will likely be in the United States in the future (using the census's middle estimates) and how the total will look broken down into select age groups.

Table 4.1 shows that all the represented age groups are projected to grow in number and contribute to the growth in total population from 309.3 million in 2010 to a projected 365.7 million in 2030. It is also apparent from the table that the fastest growing, but not the largest, aspect of the population will be those who are 65 and older. The likelihood that the retirees will grow at a fast clip is part of the problem for 2030, and we address that in greater detail later in this chapter. But first, look at the numbers. It is not as if we are moving toward an inverted demographic pyramid where the top is bigger than the base. If this were the case, as it is in some other countries, the whole economic system over a much longer period than just through the decade of the 2030s

Table 4.1   Population Growth by Age

	Number of People, in Millions		
Age Groups	2010	2020	2030
65 and older	40.5	54.6	71.6
40–64 years old	102.7	104.4	106.2
20–39 years old	83.0	88.9	92.9
<20 years old	83.2	89.0	94.9
Total	**309.3**	**336.8**	**365.7**

Source: U.S. Census Bureau.

would be under incredible strain. There would simply be far too many aging people dependent upon the economy and not enough younger folks contributing to the economy to support the aging demographic slice. Instead of finding ourselves in that circumstance, we are going to be in a position where there will be more people contributing to the economic needs of the relatively few. Clearly there is a troublesome aspect to the demographic trends depicted by Table 4.1, but it isn't fatal. We will see later that the aging trends look a lot more ominous for other countries and regions of the world.

The Census Bureau is projecting that 71.6 million people in the United States will be aged 65 and older come 2030. This estimate is consistent with the National Bureau of Economic Research's estimate of nearly 80 million aged 62 and older by 2027. We don't go from contributing to the economy to not contributing the next day. The process is gradual and cumulative. An economic switch isn't flipped when a person reaches age 65. Some may delay retirement for financial reasons. Good health could mean some people simply decide they don't want to retire at 65. There is good reason to think this might occur. We are healthier than we used to be at age 65. This is an important facet of our premise for two reasons.

One reason is the dependency ratio. The dependency ratio is derived by dividing the number of folks 65 and older by the number of people of working age. However, we maintain that people are more active and healthier in the latter half of their 60s than was previously true. This means that they are less dependent on society than they used to be. The dependency issue is probably evened out in the long run given average life expectancy is increasing, so we get to be dependent longer than was the case in generations past.

A second reason is that extrapolating the relatively healthier status of those 65 and older into the future means that one of the solutions to the aging population dilemma would be to significantly increase the retirement age beyond what is currently planned (65 to 67 years old).

We are healthy enough to work longer, and we may need to because most Americans are *not* financially prepared for retirement. If people are financially encouraged to work longer, they are less dependent upon the economy, and the government is in a position where it does not need to support them. The economic solution seems clear, but no doubt it will be extremely difficult to achieve politically. As a side note, one of the ways that the younger generations can save themselves in this regard is to increase their voter participation. The elderly vote in higher numbers as a group than the 20- to 39-year-olds do. Politicians want to be reelected. The younger voters are going to need to give politicians a reason to make the logical economic choice of raising the retirement age enough to avert the financial stress.

None of this is rocket science, with at least a partial solution to the Social Security financial woes already provided to the government and the American people by the Simpson-Bowles Report. The report was the result of a bipartisan effort to look at solutions to issues surrounding Social Security, Medicaid and Medicare, and taxes. The committee was cochaired by Alan Simpson, Republican and former senator, and Erskine Bowles, Democrat and former White House chief of staff. Although the direction the report suggested for fixing our financial woes makes sense, we think they did not go far enough and get there fast enough.

Regarding Social Security, the Simpson-Bowles Report offered the following general solutions: (1) index the retirement age to longevity, (2) reduce benefits for the middle class and the wealthy, and (3) increase the amount of income subject to the Social Security tax. Regarding point 1, they suggested increasing the retirement age to 69 by 2075. The system will be broken long before we get to 2075, so right idea but not aggressive enough. For point 2, they wanted to reduce benefits beginning in 2050. The trust funds will be broke in 2036, so why wait until 2050? Point 3 was increasing the level of income that pays the Social Security tax; we are not generally in favor of tax increases, but sometimes it has to happen. Social Security is a wealth transfer mechanism, and it is only logical to remove an artificial cap on wages subject to taxation. If you want to take from the rich to give to the poor when they retire, say so and let the American people decide.

The Simpson-Bowles Report shows that there is the possibility of a political solution to our financial woes. The good news for generation Y and younger is that census data show that voter turnout among the younger segment of the population is improving (see Table 4.2), so the potential for a political solution may be increasing.

The data presented in Table 4.2 show that we won't be swamped by hordes of people aged 65 and older in absolute terms, but remember, they are the fastest growing age bracket. Table 4.3 points this out by presenting the percentage of increase in each population segment from 2010 to 2030. Far and away, the biggest surge in the age groups is 65 and older, at 76.8 percent. That is an amazing number because, eventually, people 65 and older no longer work as much, or pay the same taxes, or make the same consumption expenditures, or consume the same amount of health care as the younger generations. There is *good* news depicted by Table 4.3 in that the slowest growing age group is the 40 to 65 tranche. This means that the baby boomers are not going to

Table 4.2   Voter Participation by Age

	2000	2004	2008
All ages	59.5	63.8	63.6
18–20 years old	31.3	44.8	44.1
21–24 years old	40.1	48.2	51.7
25–34 years old	50.5	55.7	57.0
35–44 years old	60.5	64.0	62.8
45–64 years old	67.8	69.2	69.2
65 years and older	69.6	71.0	70.3

Source: U.S. Census Bureau.

Table 4.3   Population Growth by Age Group

Age Groups	Percentage of Change 2010–2030
65 and older	76.8 percent
40–64 years old	3.4 percent
20–39 years old	11.9 percent
<20 years old	14.1 percent
Total	**18.2 percent**

Source: U.S. Census Bureau.

Table 4.4   Percent of Total Population by Age Group

Age Groups	Percentage of Total Population		
	2010	2020	2030*
65 and older	13.1 percent	16.2 percent	19.6 percent
40–64 years old	33.2 percent	31.0 percent	29.0 percent
20–39 years old	26.8 percent	26.4 percent	25.4 percent
<20 years old	26.9 percent	26.4 percent	25.9 percent
Total	**100 percent**	**100 percent**	**100 percent**

*There is a 0.1 percent rounding error if you add the 2030 column percentages.
Source: U.S. Census Bureau.

be replaced immediately by another cadre of economically dependent people.

Table 4.4 shows what percent of the total each of the age groups will comprise going forward as well as showing what the numbers were in 2010.

We see that the 65 and older age group will likely grow to be 19.6 percent of the total population by 2030. This is up from 13.1 percent in 2010. The 40- to 64-year-old group will decrease in relative importance from 33.2 percent in 2010 to 29.0 percent in 2030. By comparison, the younger generations will be stable in their relative importance. This is an important alternative means of expressing that the United States isn't becoming some massive inverted pyramid when it comes to our age groups and, therefore, why our demographic issues represent a correctable situation, whether now, during the coming Great Depression, or after the Great Depression.

It is only natural to wonder if there can be a righting of the economic ship given the rapid increase in the population aged 65 and older. If the trends were to continue in the same direction, society would indeed find it difficult to get in front of this curve and find the means to care for those 65 and older. Here is where there is some good news. The dependency ratio for the population aged 65 and older *levels off* after 2030 (at least through 2060) based on Pew Research Group projections. This is important because it means even though we will continue to gray as a society, the economic burden will not continue to mount. The Census Bureau figures are not quite as flat after 2030 as the Pew Research because the Census Bureau shows a smaller increase in the population after 2030 than Pew Research assumes. Even using census data, there is a definite and beneficial bend in the curve after 2030. You can see this point illustrated by the Pew Research Group data in Figure 4.1, which shows the elderly share of the U.S. population leveling off at

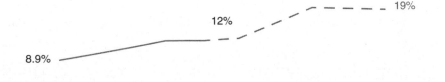

Note: Elderly are ages 65 and older. Projections for 2005–2050 indicated by broken line.

Figure 4.1   Elderly Share of U.S. Population, Actual and Projected: 1960–2050 (Percentage of Total)

Source: Pew Research Center, 2008.

about 19 percent after 2030. Census data put the figure more in the range of 20 to 21 percent.

Show Me the Money

So far, we have been looking at the numbers of people in the different age groups between now and 2030. What we need to think of besides the numbers of people is how much money the folks aged 65 and older make and how they spend their money.

Income for our purposes is more than just earned income (wages and salaries). Income is derived from the following list of sources. The 65-and-older group receives funds from all these sources:

- Wages and salaries
- Self-employment income
- Social Security and private and government retirement
- Interest, dividends, rental income, and other property income
- Unemployment and workers' compensation and veterans' benefits
- Public assistance, supplemental security income, and food stamps
- Regular contributions for support
- Miscellaneous other income

Before diving into the aggregate figures (our macroeconomic approach), keep in mind that the median income for people aged 65 and older in 2011 was $19,939. The standard of living for these people would be significantly lowered if we were to suddenly cut benefits as the only solution. Most people haven't saved enough to prepare themselves for the cash outlays they will need for maintaining their health and planned standard of living. Fortunately, it seems that people are getting the message about needing to take care of themselves and not relying on Social Security because this median income is up 10.9 percent from

10 years earlier (adjusted for inflation). We think this trend toward higher inflation-adjusted incomes provides maneuvering room for altering benefits in the future. For now, people in general depend on Social Security.

Social Security, followed by private and government retirement, make up the single largest income components for the 65-and-older group (56.6 percent based on 2011 Bureau of Labor Statistics [BLS] data). As a group, the older population naturally depends on retirement income (pensions) more than any other group, and they it earn less money than any other age group except those younger than 25. The older age groups likely hold more assets than the younger groupings and therefore derive passive cash flow in the form of interest, dividends, rental income, and other property income. This is evidenced in Table 4.5.

Although the aggregate figures in Table 4.5 are in millions of dollars, the numbers under each of the age categories are percentages of the aggregate. For instance, those 65 and older accounted for 14.4 percent of aggregate money income before taxes made in 2011.

Table 4.5   Source of Income by Age

Item	Aggregate	Younger than 25 Years	25–34 Years	35–44 Years	45–54 Years	55–64 Years	65 Years and Older
Money income before taxes	$7,787,814	2.7	15.3	21.6	25.0	21.0	14.4
Interest, dividends, rental income, and other property income	$156,669	0.6	3.3	8.3	15.2	28.3	44.3

Note: The aggregate figures are in millions of dollars. Other figures are percent of the total for each line.

Source: U.S. Census Bureau.

That same age group accounted for 44.3 percent of the income harvested from interest, dividends, rents, and other property income.

As you can see, this is a significant source of income for those 65 and older. One could argue that if we really wanted to level the playing field between those folks with assets and those without, as a society we could decide to force the aging population to sell off their assets to raise funds to pay for their own needs before being eligible to receive Social Security, Medicare, and so on. Surely such a draconian approach would be un-American in the extreme with the attendant economic effect of severely depressing asset prices for everyone. This is precisely why making Social Security benefits contingent upon wealth rather than income is so wrong.

We have seen in Table 4.5 that the 65-and-older group is not without income (fortunately!), but as a group the income is smaller than even those people who are early on in their careers (25- to 34-year-olds). We have seen that they are very dependent on retirement or pension income, which is highly susceptible to the vagaries of inflation, and on passive income. Those with an opportunity for passive income will find that this source will generally offer them some relative protection from the ill effects of inflation. It is important that the 65-and-older group spends a much higher percentage of their total income than do the other groups, with the exception of those younger than 25. This is not surprising. Populations with lower income levels tend to have less discretionary income after the staples of life are accounted for; it is also likely that the older age group simply is no longer concerned with saving for the future. Either way, a change in income for the elderly will have a much more direct effect on how much money they are able to spend. This matters in terms of the macroeconomic view via retail sales, and so on, and on the standard of living for people 65 years and older. The annual average income for people 65 and older was only 4 percent higher than their average expenditures in 2009. An environment of low interest rates (affecting income) but inflation running consistently higher than 2 percent (affecting nominal dollar spending) means that folks see their income, and therefore ability to spend, seriously eroded. We expect this trend is going to continue. It is expected to be an exacerbating factor to the business cycle recession of 2018 or 2019 and a major contributing factor to the coming Great Depression. Spending by those 65 and older accounted for 17.1 percent of total expenditures in 2012, up from 15.1 percent in 2000. The increase makes sense given the expanding size of this portion of the population. Even if we hold the total expenditure contribution flat at 17.1 percent (a very conservative assumption), a 20 percent decline in spending by the elderly could cause a 2.5 percent decline in GDP.

The elderly are going to be disproportionately hurt by inflation because it more directly affects their spending on health care and staying warm or cool. Cost increases in health care are well documented and likely to continue. Where are those 65 and older supposed to cut back to make up the difference in income growth (low) and cost of living growth (especially high for the elderly)? Food? Is that where you would like to make an adjustment?

Table 4.6 shows that there are quite a few similarities in spending between the aggregate of all age groups and those 65 and older. Food is a good example. As a percentage of total expenditures for the aggregate versus a percentage of total expenditures identified solely with those 65 and older, we see the numbers are essentially the same at 13.0 percent and 12.8 percent (data are from the 2011 BLS *Consumer Expenditure Survey*). Looking a little lower on the table, it makes sense to us that utility bills constitute a bigger chunk of total outlays for the older age group versus the aggregate, and it isn't surprising that those 65 and older spend less than the aggregate on apparel. (Anyone with teenagers would have guessed that one!)

The 65-and-older group spends less on transportation (automobile manufacturers, take note) and about the same percentage on entertainment and personal care products and services.

Table 4.6   Spending Differences and Similarities

Item	Aggregate Percentage of Total Expenditures	65 and Older Percentage of Total Expenditures
Food	13.0 percent	12.8 percent
Housing	33.8 percent	35.0 percent
Shelter	19.8 percent	18.5 percent
Utilities, fuels, and public services	7.5 percent	9.0 percent
Household operations	2.3 percent	2.8 percent
Apparel and services	3.5 percent	2.9 percent
Transportation	16.7 percent	14.7 percent
Gasoline and motor oil	5.3 percent	4.5 percent
Health care	6.7 percent	12.2 percent
Entertainment	5.2 percent	5.1 percent
Personal care products and services	1.3 percent	1.4 percent
Reading	0.2 percent	0.4 percent
Education	2.1 percent	0.6 percent
Cash contributions	3.5 percent	6.1 percent
Personal insurance and pensions	10.9 percent	5.1 percent

Source: BLS, *Consumer Expenditure Survey,* 2011.

Big differences in the relative importance of spending categories become apparent as we look toward the bottom of Table 4.6. Nearly twice as big a bite goes toward health care (12.2 percent) than is true of the aggregate (6.7 percent). Keep in mind these are out-of-pocket expenditures and do not include what governments or insurance companies are also paying. Clearly, reigning in health care costs is crucial to the financial well-being of those 65 and older.

Not surprising is that the 65-and-older group spends much less on education. However, note that although the number is small, the older age group spends double the percentage as the aggregate on reading materials (publishers that don't offer large print should take note). The older group spends much less on personal insurance and pensions, which is also to be expected. What proved to be a pleasant surprise is how much more *giving* the 65-and-older group does compared with the aggregate, with cash contributions of 6.1 percent and 3.5 percent, respectively. Indeed, the 65-and-older group was the most charitable demographic of all, surpassing even the peak earning years in terms of how much money it will give away as a percent of all expenditures. We think this is worth remembering the next time you run across the dependency ratio because apparently the older age group is prepared to give back!

Table 4.6 also points out that the decrease in standard of living that comes from inflation (discussed in Chapter 5) will affect the 65-and-older group every bit as much as the aggregate in terms of expenditures on food, utilities, shelter, and so on. Inflation hurts their income more severely than it hurts the aggregate. The aged bear a disproportionate burden when prices are escalating, especially because it is unlikely the CPI cost of living allowances applied to their retirement or pension income will keep up with the true cost of what they are buying.

Medicare and Social Security

Medicare and Social Security are two vitally important components of the social compact between the government and those 65 and older. They are also two major spending programs that the government will not be able to afford in the future, unless taxes are increased to pay for the programs or benefits are reduced (which would include extending the retirement age beyond 67). We discuss in Chapter 7 how these twin issues already involve massive dollars and that they are growing as a share of our GDP. Combined, Social Security and Medicare accounted for 38 percent of federal expenditures in 2012.

The details, the jargon, and the numbers can be overwhelming, but in its simplest form the issue is we can't afford to maintain current

Table 4.7   Benefit Costs in 2012, in Billions of Dollars

OASI	DI	HI*	SMI†
645.5	140.3	266.8	307.4

*Hospital Insurance portion of Medicare.

†Supplementary Medical Insurance portion of Medicare, which covers Parts B (physicians) and D (prescriptions).

Source: Social Security and Medicare Boards of Trustees, "A Summary of the 2013 Annual Reports," 2013.

spending trends. Table 4.7 provides some perspective to the numbers. The single biggest line item at present is Social Security, which includes Old-Age and Survivors Insurance (OASI) and Disability Insurance (DI). They totaled $785.8 billion in 2012. The Medicare total was $574.2 billion. Both numbers are growing quickly as the 65-and-older population increases in share relative to the total population.

The Social Security's DI trust fund is essentially depleted now. We are fortunate that it is the smallest of the four major categories. The fact that it has been on its way to being a completely depleted trust for years and no major structural changes are forthcoming is probably a very telling sign of things to come for the other major entitlement trusts.

The Medicare trustees estimate that the Medicare HI trust fund will be depleted by 2026. That date has slipped further into the future by a few years with recent estimates. The Affordable Care Act has been credited as part of the reason for the more distant depletion date as was an increase in tax revenues. We expect tax increases will be normal going forward and that the depletion date for HI could slip further toward 2030.

The Social Security OASI trust fund is projected to be depleted by 2036. Figure 4.2 shows very clearly that by 2036 the trust fund will be empty. Something will have to be done to maintain some level of the promised distribution to the elderly. That something could be done

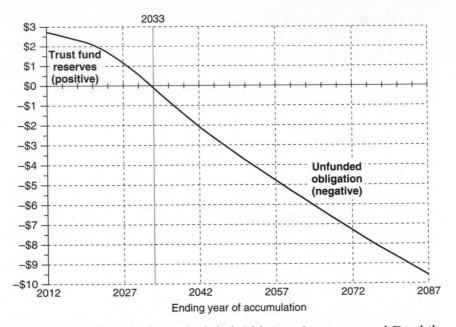

Figure 4.2 Cumulative Scheduled Old-Age, Survivors, and Disabilities Insurance Income Less Cost, from Program Inception through Years 2012–2087 (Present Value as of January 1, 2013, in Trillions)
Source: 2013 OASD Trustees Report.

now (which would be smart), or it could be in 2030 or so, which would be a contributing factor to the Great Depression of the 2030s.

Medicare SMI (Medicare Parts B and D) as a stand-alone line item is estimated to be well funded indefinitely into the future and is not seen as a causal factor for the coming Great Depression. However, if the SMI funds are raided to help balance the HI portion of Medicare, the combined trust fund will become depleted around 2033.

For the purposes of this book, the implications for the economy are in the guise of reduced benefits or higher taxes to maintain benefits. Either way, spending is affected because either the elderly will have less money to spend or younger taxpayers will have less money to spend. Remember the timeline, Medicare HI trust fund depletion of 2026 (or later), and Social Security trust fund depletion of 2033–2036. Wrap those realities up with political inertia, and you have a significant driver of the Great Depression. We are assuming that something will be done eventually to alter the course of these trends. The demographic trends are much more difficult to alter, so we are presuming that some combination of higher taxes and lower benefits will be used to effect change. We also assume that political inertia means that we will wait until we are in the midst of the financial crisis (circa 2026–2036) before effecting meaningful change. The longer we wait to correct these trends, the more painful the remedy becomes in the short term. Hence, the combination of demographics and the twin entitlements of Social Security and Medicare tie in very well with our theory that a Great Depression is coming and that its advent is probable around 2030.

Managing to Win

It is easy to become caught up in the big-picture numbers and trends and to then apply them as absolutes to ourselves at a microeconomic level. However, probably the most important word in the preceding sentence is *big*. The U.S. economy is huge. No country on the planet comes close to us in size as is discussed elsewhere in this book. Within this vast economy of ours is an amazing amount of maneuvering room for individuals. Although it may be extremely difficult or impossible to alter some of the demographic and entitlement spending trends as we head toward 2030, it is very possible for us as individuals to take action to safeguard our family's financial well-being. This, of course, would not be true if everyone, everywhere, were to read this book and take our advice. Because only a small slice of people actually will have bought this book and *acted* upon it, the freedom to outmaneuver the trends exists at a microeconomic level.

Before we delve into the list of probable winners and losers that will help us outmaneuver the demographic realities, let's take a step further into the macro perspective so that you can see why we should be glad that we are facing this future from within the United States rather than other parts of the world. Table 4.8 provides that perspective by comparing the potential 2030 demographic status of the United States with other economies.

Starting with the 65-and-older grouping, notice that India (8.9 percent), Brazil (12.2 percent), Mexico (11.5 percent), and Central America (excluding Mexico, 11.1 percent) will be considerably less gray than the United States as a percentage of their total populations. Although India's absolute number of 65 and older will be large because of the sheer size of the population, the percentages suggest that it will have a volume of people in the younger age categories sufficient to fund the needs of the elderly. The relatively small share of the population aged 65 and older at present in India is partially accounted for by a shorter life expectancy (67) than we find in most of the other countries. Russia's life expectancy is about the same as India's.

For countries with a relatively young population (e.g., Mexico and parts of Central America, such as Colombia) the issues surrounding the elderly are likely to be much less problematic in the future versus aging populations in Japan, Western Europe, and Russia. The former group may provide avenues of prosperity for businesses and individuals as they will offer some protection from this particular Great Depression driver.

On the opposite end of the spectrum, the largest percentages of elderly people are going to be found in Japan (32.2 percent), Germany (27.9 percent), and Canada (24.8 percent). Each of these countries has a significant financial problem in the future in terms of balancing taking care of the elderly and finding the means of paying for that care. Note also that what is true for Germany is true for Europe as a whole. We highlighted Germany's numbers because "as goes Germany, so goes the rest of Europe." The demographic data suggest that it is going to be incredibly difficult for Germany to continue to bail out the rest of Western Europe because of this demographic stress. We likely won't have to wait until 2030 to see this facet of the demographic trend

Table 4.8 Demographic Comparison across Countries: Estimated Percentage of Total Population (in Millions) in 2030

Age Group	United States	China	India	Europe	Germany	Brazil	Russia	Mexico	Central America*	Japan	Canada
65 and older	19.6	17.2	8.9	21.2	27.9	12.2	20.1	11.5	11.1	32.2	24.8
40–64 years old	29.0	37.9	28.9	33.3	32.9	32.7	36.8	29.7	28.6	32.8	30.8
20–39 years old	25.4	24.0	31.0	24.1	21.5	29.1	22.2	28.9	30.6	19.5	23.7
<20 years old	25.9	21.0	31.4	21.6	17.6	25.9	21.1	29.9	29.8	15.6	20.6
Total population	365.7	1,391.50	1,460.7	483.5	78.0	223.9	138.2	135.2	134.5	120.8	38.6

*Excluding Mexico.
Source: U.S. Census Bureau.

play out. However, it is clear that we cannot look to Europe to pro-vide some sort of balance to the U.S. demographic depression driver of the 2030s.

There is more to discern from Table 4.8. Take another look at China, Western Europe, Russia, Japan, and Canada. If you look at the balance of people who will be older than 40 compared with the balance who will be 30 and younger, you will see that each of these areas has an *inverted people pyramid* to contend with. Having more young people than older people has been normal through the course of human history. But declining birth rates coupled with a lack of sufficient immigration to offset the birth rates means that these five areas will have more than 50 percent of their respective populations older than 40 years of age. A very real, relative lack of young people will exist in these countries and regions in the future, with Japan at 65 percent and Germany at 60.8 percent faring the worst. Who are these countries going to tax, and at what rates will they tax them to support the aging population? These will be very contentious issues in the future, more so than we will likely have to contend with in the United States.

China and Russia are projected to have populations in the 40- to 64-year-old category, at 37.9 percent and 36.8 percent, respectively, in 2030. This is not good news as it is appreciably higher than the other countries on our chart. This means that relative to the United States post the coming depression, the demographic situation is going to worsen the most in China and in Russia. By comparison, the United States, India, Mexico, and other countries should fare much better.

We do not particularly believe the census data when it comes to Russia. Census data are calling for only a very mild absolute decline in Russia's population. We think the decline in population has the poten-tial to be much more significant than the 3 million people the census data implies. Russia is one of the few places on this planet where the death rate is higher than the birth rate, a truly remarkable and negative demographic statistic.

Following the Great Depression of the 2030s, the United States will find itself in the relatively enviable position of seeing its dependency ratio level off, likely because of an increasing death rate in the United States coupled with a fertility rate and immigration sufficient to keep our younger population growing. This leveling off in the dependency ratio is extremely important for us to find our financial footing through the depression and have the demographic means to thrive afterward. Japan, Western Europe, China, and Russia will not be as fortunate.

Probable Winners

- *People who save or contribute to their 401(k)s.* People of every demographic who create an effective combination of saving and investing will be better prepared for the coming Great Depression than those who don't because they will be able to augment government retirement and medical programs to maintain a reasonable standard of living. It is our hope that this book will engender an urgent need to do so as well as provide a how-to guide to save and invest efficaciously. Saving alone won't do the trick because inflation will eat into the value of the dollar ($1 in 2030 will buy a lot less than $1 can buy in 2014).

- *Businesses that focus on countries or regions with comparatively young populations.* Whether a business focuses on the next year or the next 10 years, expending capital and energy in China and Russia may make sense. However, if a firm is looking further down the road and looking for where the better growth percentages will be found, it will have to turn to where there is an expanding middle class, not a shrinking middle class. Those countries with inverted people pyramids are not the ones where middle class expansion will organically occur.

- *Firms that are gearing efforts toward the Latino and Hispanic segment of the population.* The Hispanic community in 2005 constituted

14 percent of the U.S. population; whites constituted 67 percent. By 2030 Hispanics will account for 29 percent of the total population, and whites will be at 47 percent. There is a tremendous surge of Hispanic culture, language, and needs coming our way that successful businesses will pay attention to if they want to gain market share and enjoy relative prosperity, even during the coming Great Depression. African Americans will be relatively constant at 13 percent of the population (same as 2005), and the Asian population will grow to 9 percent of the total from 5 percent in 2005.

- *Firms that develop niche products and services dealing with the elderly (keep in mind this slice of the pie will stop growing in the 2030-2040 decade).* Be it independent living facilities, skilled nursing homes, special dietary needs, personal care requirements, travel needs, entertainment, or whatever you can think of (the list goes on and on), catering to the needs of those 65 and older will be a growth industry between now and 2030. In the United States, the market will cease to grow as a percentage of the whole population after 2030, so expect pricing to become more competitive and the field to become more crowded beginning in the Great Depression of the 2030s. Turning to even older populations outside the United States will also prove to be a winning strategy.

(Potential) Losers

- *Generation Y (born 1981–2000).* Our concern for generation Y regarding the 2030s depression is twofold. One, it is going to have to care for a disproportionately large elderly population. This is both costly (financially and emotionally) and time-consuming. Two, it will be entering its peak earning years around the time the United States and the rest of the globe is slipping into what looks to be a decade-long depression. Unless they are especially prepared (another reason for this book), they will become the economically lost generation.

- *People 65 and older who don't create a nest egg.* There is a coming stress point where retirement and medical benefits will be reduced, be delayed, or cost more. Any way you look at it, people who are relying on the system to provide for them in their elder years are likely to experience a significant drop in their standard of living.

- *Incumbent politicians.* The political choices that face us between now and 2030 are going to range from painful to dangerous. In the end, doing the economically right thing is not likely to win votes for reelection. Additionally, anyone in office as we head into a Great Depression is going to have a difficult time justifying why they should be reelected. Politics as a career between 2025–2034 is something generation Y should avoid if they are going to try to earn a consistent wage during the depression.

- *Taxpayers.* Reduce benefits or raise taxes will be the primary choices confronting politicians. The path of least resistance will be to increase taxes on the rich. That is an interesting concept because politicians will get to decide who the rich are. Most likely they will construe the rich as those with higher incomes or with substantial assets. The rich today pay most of the taxes the government receives. Get ready to pony up even more money in the future.

5 A World That Doesn't Remember Inflation

New Management and Investment Thought Processes Required

O ur research indicates that *inflation* will be one of the most significant depression drivers for 2030. It won't necessarily be that hyperinflation will occur in the United States or in other major economies; however, such extreme inflation does not *need* to occur for us to have a significant problem.

This chapter looks at some of the potential sources and manifestations of inflation in the coming years and the dire result of this trend for both the economy *and* our personal well-being. Our major concern is that one of the historical consequences of prolonged inflation—namely, a significant economic downturn—will be very difficult, if not impossible, to avoid in this cycle. Inflation leads to imbalances, poor decisions, a lower standard of living, and for our purposes, severe business cycle declines powerful enough in magnitude to be called depressions.

Fortunately, inflation is probably the easiest technical fix of all the depression drivers we have thought about as a precursor to the coming

Great Depression, especially since we are still in the early days. And like most things, *preventing* inflation is easier than ridding our economy of it once it is here. However, eradicating inflation requires a trade-off that does not seem viable at this time: sacrificing some near-term gain to avoid long-term pain. It is human nature to forestall pain in the hopes we may never have to face it. The willingness to accept some pain today to avoid potentially more in the future is not a social contract politicians and the majority of the people they represent are willing to make. This is true in the United States and elsewhere in the world—and we all have to live with the consequences of this choice.

We have not seen persistent, problematic inflation in the global economy for some time. In the United States, inflation peaked in 1980 and has become less of a problem since. Indeed, the fear of inflation was replaced with a fear of deflation. The ongoing deflation dilemma in Japan seemed to reinforce this fear in other nations. Instead of seeing prices go up, we witnessed price erosion, which drove the need to become more efficient, become more productive, always find better ways, find low-cost alternatives, and take greater risks. At the time, it served a useful economic purpose.

However, the deflation threat is now overstated, and the inflation threat is not given enough credence. The very fact that it has been approximately 25 years since inflation peaked gives rise to the specter of its return as a new generation of managers and owners are coming into their own—a new generation that has known deflation but not persistent, problematic inflation. When you have been in the pressure cooker of price erosion long enough that the collective memory of price inflation is no longer prominent or doesn't exist at all, the prospect of inflation actually begins to seem a lot more benign, if not downright beneficial, compared to the deflation you've known. Of course, the best outcome would be *price stability*, where neither inflation nor deflation is the predominant theme. However, that's simply not a long-term probability. Economies are pendulums that swing from one extreme to the next. Deflation dissipates and is eventually replaced with inflation, which will inevitably give way to another round of deflation. This seesaw pattern is evident in the historical data gleaned from all over the world.

The shift to a secular inflationary trend will bring terms, such as *cost of living allowances* (COLAs), and debates about how best to measure inflation and protect retirees from the effects of inflation back to the economic dialogue. COLAs become a routine fabric of economic life during periods of inflation. Let's assume that the Consumer Price Index (CPI) registers a 4 percent rate of inflation. Benefits that the government pays, including Social Security, will routinely be adjusted upward by the same amount, 4 percent, but after the fact. Firms will tend to do the same with employees and assume that the minimum pay increase employees will get is 4 percent to compensate them for the reality of inflation eating away at their standard of living. Such intentions are noble—but the reality is that the benefit or pay increase is being paid out on what *was* occurring, not what *is* occurring.

During the prolonged period of inflation we see coming, it is likely that the *current* rate of inflation will be higher than what transpired the previous year (unless the economy slips into business cycle decline). This means that retirees and those employees who have just received a COLA will be *marginally* better off. However, they will still be financially worse off than they were before the inflation trend started—and worse off than they were in the preceding year as the inflationary years roll on.

Governments must realize that as protected as they think retirees and beneficiaries of other programs will be from the vagaries of inflation by virtue of these COLAs, they are still putting people in a losing situation by virtue of allowing inflation to take root in the first place. Business leaders must understand that (1) their employees are not worth the 4 percent increase in cost just because they have lived through a year of inflation; (2) their employees will still demand even higher wages in the future; and (3) products and services sold into a population who depends on COLAs for increases in disposable personal income will be in a situation in which hoped for customers will become increasingly unable to afford what businesses are selling.

The elements described earlier make it vital for business leaders to train their employees continuously to increasingly higher levels of productivity so that they are *worth* the COLA they just received. It also means that employees are always going to want more than leaders just gave them during periods of prolonged inflation. Additionally, higher margins are to be made selling upscale products and services to people who aren't dependent on COLAs to (seemingly) maintain their standard of living.

We are currently transitioning out of deflation and into inflation on a global scale—particularly in those economies with the best long-term growth prospects, such as those with a growing population and a rich natural resource base, including Australia, India, and the United States. The transition process should affect how we run our business and how we invest. It requires that we make some decisions that might initially seem counterintuitive based on our experiences and memory. The welfare of the young and old alike will change from what is currently perceived as probable once inflation has run its course.

A significant shift in mind-set will occur over the next 10 to 15 years, a transition in thinking that will be difficult for business leaders who've graduated from the lean and mean school of business. History shows that it is normal for businesses to rely on price increases to manage inflationary pressures and rising costs instead of continuously striving for efficiencies and superior performance results. This may sound very strange to those who cut their teeth in the 1990s and 2000s, when efficiencies became the mantra, capital was relatively cheap, and we invested in maintaining or reclaiming world-class status as a service provider or a manufacturer. After a decade of inflation and constantly growing interest rates, the course of least resistance becomes raising prices rather than risking seemingly relatively expensive capital improvements. The closer we get to the inflation peak and the coming Great Depression, the more tempting the easy course of raising prices will become. When the price cycle turns from inflation to disinflation or deflation as a consequence of the Great Depression, companies that relied on the raising prices tactic will find themselves unable to compete in very short order. The firms with the strongest, most efficient processes will have the best opportunity to manage the significant decline. Raising prices instead of combating inflationary pressures via efficiencies is akin to the frog that is put into a pot of water that is slowly brought to a boil. The frog will not think to jump out until it is far too late. Don't be the economic equivalent of that frog.

As inflation compounds through multiple business cycles, it becomes even more essential to know when and how to get or make price commitments. Prices tend to rise and decline in concert with the general business cycle but on a slightly lagging basis, something we can use to our advantage. When the leading indicators are pointing toward a recovery, it pays to lock in input prices (material, money, and labor) before the business cycle pushes prices higher.

Take a one-year lock-in from your suppliers at a minimum; three years (for example, in the case of a labor contract) would be better. Your suppliers may want to build in an escalator to adjust prices if the period is uncomfortably long for them—so choose your escalator wisely.

When dealing with suppliers, try to select a price index that will tend to understate the real price increase. You may try to use the over-all Producer Price Index (PPI) in a business-to-business situation. For instance, in the recovery year of 2004, the PPI rose 4.2 percent, versus the more specific Manufacturing Producer Price Index gain of 9.1 percent through the same period. The best escalator to use would be the CPI, which had a 2004 increase of only 3.3 percent. You want to negotiate for the index that will help you keep your costs down. Over a three-year period, the PPI rose 11.1 percent, the Manufacturing Producer Price index was up 27.0 percent, and the CPI was up 8.1 percent.

Picking the right escalator can make a material impact on the bottom line.

Don't lock in prices when your customers request that you do so. But if you have to, make sure you pick the escalator that will afford you the most protection. Using the indexes cited previously, negotiate with your customers so that you end up using the Manufacturing Producer Price Index, which will yield you a 27.0 percent price increase over three years versus just 8.1 percent if you used the much more common CPI.

Inflation comes in several forms and stems from numerous causes. There is asset price inflation, which is most easily identified with loose monetary policy. Think of the U.S. housing bubble of 2006 and the global bubble in stock prices in the latter half of the 1990s, 2003 through 2007, and 2010 through 2013. There is also run-of-the-mill price inflation, which can come because of labor prices increasing. It may start with commodity prices rising, consumer expectations of higher prices, or government policies. For example, as we write this, the government of Japan is trying to reignite inflation, and the United States is maintaining a course of action that clearly fears deflation and high unemployment more than future inflation. Europe is seeing no serious signs of inflation as it struggles to rebound from the financial issues of 2008. China has no clear picture of inflation that it shares with the rest of the world. India is contending with inflation of 10.7 percent in late 2013 while its economy struggles to grow. Although we are clearly a global economy, the preceding shows that there are competing sovereign interests at work that make a globally coherent policy about inflation impossible to achieve and adhere to. In the end, the larger economies will hold sway over the smaller ones. For better or worse, the United States' propensity to inflating its economy is going to bring inflationary pressures to bear on other countries.

Inflation is rather straightforward from a business perspective: costs are going up. It could be materials, labor, power, taxes, or social costs, but something is escalating the cost of producing the good or service one is in business to produce. This type of inflation is arguably the most painful in the long term. It also happens to be the one with which people today are least familiar. This isn't the short-run inflation Japan has in mind when it tries to stimulate some domestic demand; rather, it is what happens after an initial surge in inflation occurs and the spiral catches hold. Then, a broader follow-on inflation replaces the initial pulse of higher prices.

This broader inflation is not simply that business costs are going up; *consumer prices* are also rising. What makes the inflation tendency so problematic is that a very vicious self-perpetuating spiral develops. Because consumers must pay more, we demand more in the form of wages to compensate. We also want to buy what we want *now*, before prices go even higher. Because of this pressure—and particularly in places such as the United States that have a shortage of skilled labor—wages go up. This of course drives business costs even higher. Now, because *expectations* have shifted—and people have presumed that prices will indeed be going higher—businesses are able to raise prices to accommodate their higher costs. Profits go up in nominal dollar terms (not adjusted for inflation), thereby hiding the economic pain of inflation from producers. Higher wages also hide the difficulty of inflation from wage earners as well.

It is a vicious spiral, to be sure: higher prices lead us to want higher wages, which leads to price increases, which loops back to wanting higher wages again. This eventually leads to some real problems for business leaders, investors, and individuals. However, it also presents some real opportunities along the way.

Before we delve further into probable sources of inflation, we need to talk a little shop. As economists, it is always tempting to talk about real growth in new orders, retail sales, wages, and so on. The *real* comes into play when economists adjust the *stated* price of an order, sale, wage, and so forth by changes in inflation. The *stated* value looks at nominal values and prices—and people live in a nominal world. They know whether the value of their home goes up, how much more or less the items of life cost, and whether they have gotten a raise. Over time, people recognize that the raise may or may not have been able to maintain their previous standard of living. Our research at ITR Economics has shown that the majority of people make decisions based on nominal values—at least for the short term. However, if inflation persists over a long period, real growth has to come back into consideration if we are going to anticipate what certain outcomes may be.

You can also see the difference between real and stated in another context: the difference between the *officially registered inflation rate* and what people are *actually experiencing*.

Remember when oil reached $134 per barrel in mid-2008? Food prices went up, too, and real estate prices were coming down; things became tight for a lot of people, even though the *official* inflation number was low. I (Alan) remember one young lady telling me that she could not fill her car with gas, pay the mortgage, make the car payment, buy food, and pay her credit cards all in the same month anymore. I asked her if she had lost a job, and she said no, that she worked 60 hours a week at two jobs. Then I asked when she had last gotten a raise. She quickly turned angry and told me that it had been over a year!

I explained that the problem was not her or anything she'd done. Inflation had simply come along and stolen her standard of living—and she could do little about it. In less than three minutes, I had diagnosed the problem and offered no help at all, fulfilling my role as an economist. She then looked at me and said, "But *Dad*, what am I going to do?!" I said I did not know.

A very real consequence of this situation is that my daughter was angry—and angry employees are not good for your business or mine. Your employees will feel angry and frustrated, too. They are under stress and they will take it out on their employers, even if it is not the employers' fault. Employees will answer the phone on the fourth ring and not the first, walk slower to pick up the part, drive slower to the bank; any number of small inefficiencies will creep in, and your profits will reflect it. It is imperative that we adequately compensate the A and B players for the sake of efficiency and to keep them from taking all their training and knowledge to a competitor who offers to pay them more.

Inflation's Impacts

Inflation robs a population of its standard of living by reducing currency's purchasing power—sometimes, slowly and insidiously. It might even be something that people initially perceive as beneficial, like getting a hit of morphine when in pain. The shot is necessary. But the pain returns and they need another hit. And another. Unless people address the pain's underlying source, it is likely to get worse, so they need even more morphine—until finally the system can tolerate no more.

There are three ways that inflation negatively affects an economy:

1. Reduced savings

2. A lower standard of living

3. Higher unemployment

Inflation's impact on savings means that many people heading into retirement won't have enough in their nest egg to meet their desired standard of living needs. For instance, $100,000 in the bank today will buy x amount of goods and services. In 17 years, that same $100,000 will by x amount of goods and services minus the effects of inflation. The $100,000 savings will hypothetically be worth only $70,932 because a dollar just doesn't buy what it used to, assuming an average annual inflation rate of just 2 percent higher than the nominal rate of return on investment between 2013 and 2030, for instance, a rate of return that averages 8 percent but an inflation rate that averages 10 percent. We talk more about this later in this chapter, but it is an example of why at times we will use *nominal*, and sometimes we will use *real*. The purpose isn't to confuse but rather illustrate probable behavioral trends based on how people really think and react. Nominally, a person will have $100,000 in 2030, but in terms of what it can buy, it will be worth only $70,932. Retirees end up buying less than they either thought they would or thought they could. Either way, their future standard of living has decreased.

The reduced-savings phenomenon also comes into play because we want to spend more *today* rather than save to buy at the later date. We want immediate gratification anyway, but once you add the incentive that prices will be higher in the future, we have the perfect cocktail for buying, until the glass is empty. When you perceive that the suit, car, or piece of equipment you want or need is going to cost you more next year, it is rational to want to purchase it as soon as possible. So we use credit to make this happen.

This process is a double-edged sword. For consumers, it is a long-run problem (not saving for that rainy day or for retirement), but for businesses, it creates a sense of "needing to buy" in customers that is hard to beat! Businesses enjoy an increase in consumer demand because of escalating prices (consumers want it *now*) and because those higher retail prices enable businesses to cover higher unit costs stemming from raw material prices, labor, taxes, and so on. This sounds like a great period for top-line growth after 30 years of price stability or deflation. Except then our workforce wants a raise, or more to the point, *another* raise because their cost of living is going up.

Even if inflation didn't erode the dollar's basic purchasing power, we likely are not saving enough for our medical needs. Fidelity Benefits Consulting estimates that a couple retiring in 2013 will need $220,000 to cover medical expenses during retirement—a figure that does not consider costs associated with nursing homes. Unfortunately, 48 percent of those 55 to 64 years old surveyed thought they would need just $50,000. The lack of sufficient savings for medical needs in retirement could have a serious negative impact on the standard of living for a big chunk of baby boomers.

Although inflationary forces lead to various experiences of a lower standard of living, we break it down to two additional ways: (1) you keep your job but can't afford steak, so you end up buying more hamburger; or (2) you lose your job. In either scenario, you end up with cheap hamburger and more starches instead of relatively expensive fruits, vegetables, and so on. Anyone whose pay was cut because of the 2008–2009 Great Recession in a way experienced the long-term effects of inflation. In the blink of an eye, his or her income became smaller and prices remained relatively fixed. The effect is not much different from when prices are going up and your wages aren't going up as fast as the price structure is. The way to make ends meet in the Great Recession— as it will be in the future—is to substitute cheaper goods; perhaps those goods are less durable and of lower quality, but you learn to make do. Remember, you experience the same substitution phenomenon in a period of inflation because your income is stagnant relative to the cost of the goods and services you want. Your fixed-income budget may allocate $200 a week for food, but that $200 will buy less food as time goes by if food prices are going up by 4 percent a year and your budget stays the same. The trend of less steak and more hamburger signifies a reduction in the standard of living.

But why would inflation be a reason that you would lose your job? Simply put, you have become *too expensive* relative to alternative technology or other labor sources. A company decides that a certain piece of equipment can do your job in a more cost-effective manner, or a worker in some other part of the country—or the world—can perform your function as well as you can, or at least well enough to get by. Wages are sometimes the means by which labor prices itself out of the market as workers in the United States experienced in the 1990s. (The long-term relationship between inflation and unemployment is described via the Phillips Curve in the Appendix.)

Our concern for 2030–2040 is the lasting effects of prolonged inflation. We are about to see the world embark on a prolonged inflationary trend, the five reasons for which are enumerated in the following section. Like a fire that we mistakenly think is a controlled burn but actually grows into a dangerous conflagration, once started, the inflation fires can be fueled by events we did not anticipate—events that are beyond our control. If the inflation fire spreads, we have a situation similar to the state of the economy from 1965–1980. Painful and disruptive inflation will cycle higher and higher even as the Fed seeks to control it, and each cycle up leads to higher unemployment. People become too expensive. The cost of capital is fixed at the time of purchase, so we will swap people out for technology or will source the work where labor costs are less.

Inflation resulting in higher and higher levels of unemployment is a major economic threat that could contribute significantly to the coming Great Depression. The threat exists because unemployed people spend less money and thereby reduce the demand for durable and nondurable consumer goods. This reduction in demand leads to slower activity and eventual layoffs, first at wholesale distributors and then at manufacturers. A downward spiral in employment slowly takes shape that is hard to break. The other contributing factor to the depression is that state and federal expenditures for unemployment insurance will eventually move aggressively higher, straining government coffers and most likely forcing a situation where increased borrowing becomes necessary.

Five Sources of Inflation

Money Supply Growth: The Fuel

One tried-and-true way to create inflation is to expand an economy's money supply rapidly. From Spain's importation of gold following Columbus's voyage, to Mr. Greenspan and Dr. Bernanke's printing presses, we know that this approach creates some sort of inflation. It could be *general price inflation* or come in the form of an *asset price bubble.* It is hard to predict specifically where an asset price bubble will occur; however, it isn't too difficult to spot one once it becomes dangerous.

Of course, economics is not an exact discipline. Asset price bubbles seem to occur in lieu of general price inflation, perhaps because the right match hasn't been struck or because other circumstances were not sufficiently present to turn a problem in a particular asset class—such as housing or stocks—into something that goes viral. Whether we strike the right igniter for the right circumstances or not, the fuel source for some form of inflation has consistently been overly aggressive money supply expansion.

Both forms of inflation are damaging, but asset price bubbles tend to occur over a shorter period. General price inflation takes longer to develop, is more insidious, and is tolerated longer. For this reason, it frequently leads to extended periods of correction through recession, depression, or another round of deflation.

Recent history shows that rapid money supply expansion is associated with escalating stock prices. Monetary expansion seems to enable asset price bubbles, and expansion periods in the money supply tie in with significant upside activity in the stock market. The logic for why this is the case is straightforward: when you increase the supply of money, you increase the capability for the purchase of any given asset. If the herd focuses on the stock market, you get a robust ascent in prices and total market capitalization. But once you remove the stimulation of easy money, the asset price or total market capitalization loses its air and a bear market ensues. You can't assume that the next asset price bubble will again be in the stock market; however, it's not necessarily a bad bet to make.

When you see an asset price bubble develop, jump on. Then keep a very close watch on the source of the liquidity that is puffing up those assets. Pull the parachute and enjoy the profits when you see the wind changing. A bubble is essentially logical in origin; there's too much easy money. But emotional fervor seems to become an important driver of sustaining the trend, even after the stimulus is removed. You can try to time the market high if you think you are good at reading emotional tea leaves. Most of us are not going to be good at that. So pull the rip cord when the logic component is removed instead of being greedy about the last couple hundred feet of ascent you might be able to get out of the market.

In the next section, we look at some potential precipitators of general price inflation (the matches for the fire of inflation).

Domestically Sourced Inflation: Health Care

There are numerous ways to measure inflation, most of which have merit. Most businesspeople will use either the CPI or a PPI. Economists and government analysts tend to want to use the gross domestic product (GDP) price deflator. We are going to use the CPI as our primary tool. We will discuss the PPI as a potential tool you can use in the future to help mitigate the negative effects of inflation upon your business. We acknowledge that the CPI is an imperfect inflation gauge, and it is not a cost of living index; however, it is widely used, readily available, and frequently quoted. The Bureau of Labor Statistics, part of the U.S. Department of Labor, both compiles and publishes the CPI and the PPI. Figure 5.1 illustrates inflation by looking at the year-over-year increase in the monthly CPI.

The graphic shows that inflation reached its highest point in 1980 at 14.6 percent, was relatively tame for the 1990s, and has been more volatile but averaged a lower number over the past 10 years or so. It is the period from the mid-1960s through 1980 that may provide us with some idea as to what may develop within the economy in the coming years—except this time, the inflation trend will not culminate in a business cycle decline like what occurred in the early 1980s. Something worse is bound to happen, given the other depression drivers of demographics (see Chapter 4) and government finances (see Chapter 6).

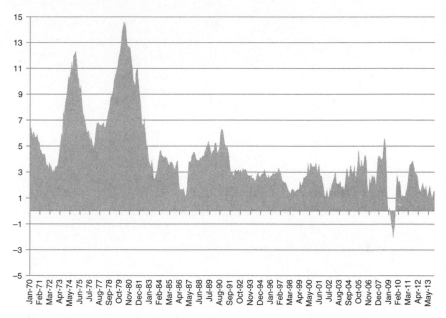

Figure 5.1   Consumer Price Index—12/12 Rate of Change

Source: Raw data provided by the Bureau of Labor Statistics; rate-of-change calculated by ITR Economics.

We are concerned not only with general inflation but also with health care inflation because of the demographics. Figure 5.2, which displays information from 1960 to today, compares the trend in the monthly CPI to the monthly index of the medical care component of the CPI.

Both trends were relatively benign through the mid-1960s but began to pick up momentum in the latter half of the 1960s and persisted until 1980. Probably not coincidentally as regards the medical care index, Medicaid and Medicare were introduced into the economy in 1965. Figure 5.2 shows that it has been normal for the medical care index to grow faster than the overall CPI, something we can easily observe from the graph because both series are plotted on a logarithmic scale. This long-standing trend is going to continue despite the best intentions of the Affordable Care Act (also known as Obamacare)—something we presume to be the case based on the logic

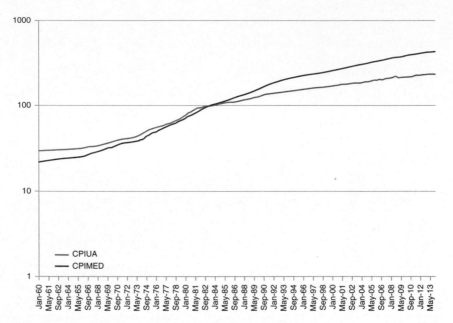

Figure 5.2   Consumer Price Index to Medical Care Consumer Price Index

Source: Bureau of Labor Statistics.

of supply and demand. When demand grows faster than supply, higher prices ensue. Nowadays, demand is escalating with an increase in the size of the population with stronger growth in the aging population and the increasing number of people who will have access to health care. The only way to at least temporarily change this paradigm is to make the government the sole purchaser of all things health care, which is a position that we do not advocate as Austrian-leaning economists. We also predict ongoing escalation in health care costs despite the intentions of the Affordable Care Act, based on the universal health insurance experience of Massachusetts.

One could argue that we should also isolate and examine the inflation trend for food because of its ubiquitous qualities. However, this is not necessary for several reasons. First, historically, food inflation has very closely matched that of the overall CPI. Second, the elderly don't spend a significantly different amount of their total expenditures on food compared with other age groups (see Chapter 4). And finally, the application of technologies has proved the Malthusian theory wrong ever since it was first proposed in 1798 (see Chapter 2).

It's no surprise that we want to live longer; in many cases, we want medicine to make up for unhealthy lifestyles. People demand it—and the government has not found a way to refuse these demands. As long as the cost of health care doesn't affect our wallets directly, we don't really care about how much any given procedure or pill costs. That is the flip side of insurance, whether private or public: it insulates consumers from feeling the full effects of rising health care costs except to the extent that they see their health insurance premiums or deductibles rising. Businesses and governments have increasingly borne the increasing cost of health care. That may change in the future—and not for the better from the consumer's perspective, as businesses insist on employees sharing more in the cost and as governments find they are unable to fund benefits at current levels.

Figure 5.3 shows the cumulative percent change in health expenditures in terms of the immediate source of the dollars used to pay the bill from 2000 through 2011, compliments of the Kaiser Family Foundation. The biggest percent increases are under Medicare and Medicaid. We delve into the impact this will have on our future when we look into U.S. debt in a later chapter. The third highest percentage is from private health insurance, and the smallest is from consumer out-of-pocket costs. Although not the largest percent change, the increase has apparently been painful to many, especially as we transition through a period of high unemployment and the beginning of the Affordable Care Act in 2014–2016. The out-of-pocket percentage has increased faster than our income over that period. The upward trend is going to continue and likely get worse. And the consequence will be a need to devote more of our income to paying for more expensive health care in the future.

It is not that individuals have not been asked to shoulder some of the burden; however, they certainly have not covered the lion's share

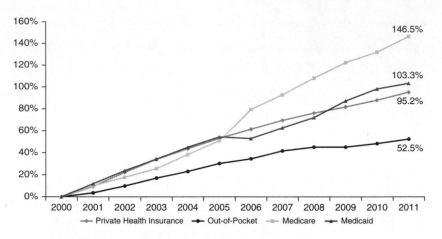

NOTE: This figure omits national health spending, which belongs in the categories of Other
Public Insurance Programs, Other Third Party Payers and Programs, Public Health Activity,
and Investment, and which together represent about 20 percent of total national health
spending in 2011. Medicare and Medicaid were enacted in 1965; by January 1970, all states
but two were participating in Medicaid.

Figure 5.3   Cumulative Percent Change in National Health
Expenditures, by Selected Sources of Funds, 2000–2011

Source: Kaiser Family Foundation calculations using NHE data from Centers for
Medicare and Medicaid Services, Office of the Actuary, National Health Statistics
Group, at www.cms.hhs.gov/NationalHealthExpendData (see Historical; National
Health Expenditures by type of service and source of funds, CY 1960-2011; file
nhe2011.zip).

of the increasing costs. One place where businesses and consumers *can*
agree is that health insurance premiums are higher—and the financial
burden that businesses and consumers have borne is cause for concern, especially as the trend continues. Figure 5.4 shows the cumulative
increase in health insurance premiums. Health insurance premiums
are up 180 percent from 1999 through 2012, according to the Kaiser
Family Foundation. The worker's contribution to cover health insurance premiums is up 172 percent through that same time. (The difference of 8 percentage points is the additional cost burden that has
been placed on businesses in that same period.) Notice in Figure 5.4
that the increases in premiums and worker contributions have been

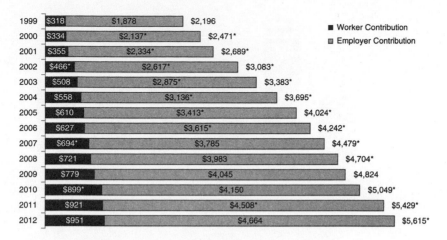

Year	Worker Contribution	Employer Contribution	Total
1999	$318	$1,878	$2,196
2000	$334	$2,137*	$2,471*
2001	$355	$2,334*	$2,689*
2002	$466*	$2,617*	$3,083*
2003	$508	$2,875*	$3,383*
2004	$558	$3,136*	$3,695*
2005	$610	$3,413*	$4,024*
2006	$627	$3,615*	$4,242*
2007	$694*	$3,785	$4,479*
2008	$721	$3,983	$4,704*
2009	$779	$4,045	$4,824
2010	$899*	$4,150	$5,049*
2011	$921	$4,508*	$5,429*
2012	$951	$4,664	$5,615*

*Estimate is statistically different from estimate for the previous year shown (p<.05).

Figure 5.4   Average Annual Worker and Employer Contributions and Total Premiums for Single Coverage, 1999–2012

Source: Kaiser/HRET Survey of Employer-Sponsored Health Benefits, 1999–2012.

far greater than nominal earning growth (gross income) and overall inflation.

The percent increase shows one story; the dollars emphasize a different point. In 2012, the average employer contribution to health insurance premiums came out to $4,664 per worker, but the average worker contribution was $951. From 1999 through 2012, average worker contributions went up $633 per annum, and the employer portion went up $2,786 per worker in the same period. The employer's increase was tolerable, as long as productivity and efficiency improvements continued to make each employee more valuable.

But true innovations and productivity and efficiency enhancements are not a *given* going forward. There is cyclicality to these events. If we aren't able to employ new technologies in the workplace (think more stringent European-style labor laws as a reason why that might be difficult going forward), businesses will be forced to either push the increasing premiums through to consumers (inflation) or pass off the costs to their workers. This will incite an erosion of personal disposable income that leads to pressure for greater wage increases from the

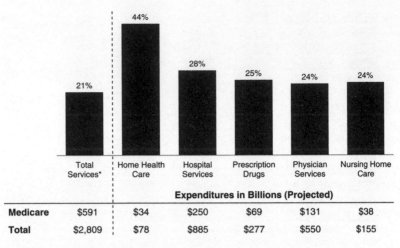

	Total Services*	Home Health Care	Hospital Services	Prescription Drugs	Physician Services	Nursing Home Care
			Expenditures in Billions (Projected)			
Medicare	$591	$34	$250	$69	$131	$38
Total	$2,809	$78	$885	$277	$550	$155

NOTE: Total also includes dental care, durable medical equipment, other professional services, and other personal health care/products.

Figure 5.5   Medicare's Share of National Personal Health Expenditures, by Type of Service, 2012

Source: Centers for Medicare and Medicaid Services, Office of the Actuary, National Health Expenditure Projections 2011–2021, June 2012.

workers, also leading to inflation. If the productivity curve is indeed flattening, as some have argued, then the result will be a higher rate of inflation.

A final thought before we leave the issue of health care inflation behind us: although the funding of Medicare is an important topic regarding our outlook for the Great Depression that lies ahead, as is the potential decrease in benefits, Figure 5.5 shows that Medicare is covering only a minority of the health care bill in the United States.

We can see here that Medicare covers only 21 percent of the national personal health expenditures. Private insurance and savings have to make up the rest for many people, including those in the 65-and-older group. Savings is particularly important as a means of covering health care costs for retirees. As we have seen, most people likely don't have enough in savings to cover their medical needs in retirement. That reality is compounded by the fact that the purchasing power of their savings nest egg is eroded year after year by inflation. Members of generation Y should take note and serve in the military to get a pension plus affordable health insurance when they retire if they want to avoid a similar fate.

Domestically Sourced Inflation: Going Green

Wanting to save the planet from harm is a laudable goal. However, "going green" without giving thought to who will bear the costs for doing so is *not* so virtuous. A case in point is electricity. Concern for the environment has already driven up the price of electricity—and it looks like a trend that's going to continue. These higher electricity costs are disproportionately borne by lower-income groups, including the elderly living on a fixed income. Utility bills account for a higher proportion of all expenditures for those 65 and older. The same logic applies to lower-income households. In this way, going green amounts to a regressive environmental tax. Keep in mind that a growing number of us are going to find ourselves in that 65-and-older fixed-income category.

Mounting electricity costs because of our quest for alternative sources is a well-documented trend. Whether it's in Germany or Florida, the cost of something so fundamental to life is higher than it otherwise would have to be. We aren't arguing against the green movement; we merely think there should be a balanced understanding as to its real costs. Consider the domino effect here: the rising price of electricity means the cost of running the neighborhood supermarket, local factory, the air-conditioning in offices, and so on are all going up. And the businesses bearing these costs will have to find ways to pass them along to their customers, making the inflationary impact in a direct business-to-consumer relationship quite evident. It also happens in business-to-business relationships. At the end of the supply chain in any scenario is the eventual consumer who will have to pay the higher price for the power needed to supply or produce products.

Anyone who has had to replace an old central air-conditioning system with a new one has certainly encountered a kind of inflation. Environmental regulations have dictated phasing out the old Freon. Not that doing away with the old Freon was in and of itself bad, but did the environmental lobby consider the financial impact it would have on families and the companies that make our GDP? It is inflation when services and things cost more and you receive no measurable or relevant performance improvement from that service or product (your house is no cooler).

Another example of a trade-off between environmental concerns and building potential inflation into the economic system is ethanol made from corn, as it is in the United States. The government has mandated that ethanol be blended into the fuel mix in the United States. Yet the government's own studies show that there is a 3 to 4 percent decrease in miles per gallon (MPG) versus the use of straight gasoline—and the figures get worse the higher the ethanol content. There is a 25 to 35 percent drop in fuel economy with E85 fuel (85 percent ethanol), and the reason is simple; the BTU (British thermal unit) content of ethanol is less than it is for gasoline. Although one could argue that the trade-off in MPG for ethanol makes sense, Cornell University findings show that for every gallon of ethanol produced, 1.4 gallons of equivalent energy are necessary to produce the ethanol, versus 0.15 gallons used in the manufacture of every gallon of gasoline. Universities other than Cornell have reviewed and substantiated these data. All have found the ratio of energy-in to energy-out to be *economically unjustifiable*, meaning that it is wasteful and therefore inflates prices relative to no ethanol. If ethanol is beneficial to reduce greenhouse gases (which some would dispute), we must recognize the economic cost of choosing to go down this path.

The United States is the world's number one producer of ethanol. We produced 13.9 billion gallons of the stuff (again primarily corn based) in 2011. Brazil was number two at 5.6 billion gallons—less than half. So it's clear that the United States is significantly invested in this endeavor. According to White Environmental Associates, every gallon of ethanol has the effect of removing 53 cents from the Federal Highway Trust Fund because of special tax breaks. Our roads and bridges nonetheless need money to avoid dangerous disrepair. Because ethanol is draining funds away from the Highway Trust Fund, the money must come from elsewhere—such as general tax revenues or, more onerously, from the government eventually printing more money to make up for the shortfall.

And let's not ignore what has been going on with corn prices in the United States while the ethanol movement has prospered. Except for severe weather disruptions, corn futures prices were relatively stable from 1985 through mid-2006, going as low as $1.47 per bushel to highs of $2.78 per bushel. Since mid-2006, corn prices have risen as high as $8.07 per bushel (monthly data). Although weather has continued to affect the corn prices' ups and downs, it would be difficult to argue that the *nearly threefold increase* in peak price is unrelated to the creation of a new and significant source of demand for the crop. These higher corn prices find their way into numerous everyday edible products. *That's* inflationary.

And it won't stop here. In our otherwise noble quest to be green, our Congress has mandated that the United States produce 36 billion gallons of ethanol annually by 2022. The slight problem here is that gasoline consumption in the United States is improving because fuel efficiency in gasoline engines is improving. So will we be forced to use higher ethanol blends that drive down fuel efficiency? Stranger things have happened.

Let's also remember that inflation leads to *a decrease in the standard of living*. Although studies vary, at least some evidence suggests that ethanol-based gasoline shortens the life span of small engines that do not have an oxygen sensor. The solutions are to buy an additive, which increases the cost of running that small engine; replace the engine more often; or install oxygen sensors on these small engines. All of these constitute costs consumers bear for the same output as before. Although we have laudable goals to be sure, they are nonetheless inflationary.

Domestically Sourced Inflation: Labor Prices

Higher commodity prices (think heating oil and gasoline) create one-off inflation. They cause a bump in prices that consumers generally must bear—or do without the commodity. The process goes viral when labor prices begin to rise because of the one-off reduction in living standards or a relative shortage of labor. We have lived through a long period of negative pressure on labor prices in this country and on this planet, so it is difficult to remember or conceive of this relationship of labor price increases being sustained. The current era of downward pressure on labor prices started in the early 1980s and is concluding as we speak. The increasing globalization of our economy at least partially drove it.

Some argue that based on the experience of the past 20 to 30 years it is highly unlikely we will see wage inflation, particularly at a time when unemployment is relatively high. These people maintain that the high unemployment rate is indicative of a labor pool that employers can readily draw upon to satisfy demand. If demand and supply are in equilibrium, prices in the form of wages do not rise. If supply is equal to, or exceeds, demand; no wage inflation will ensue. However, it's too simplistic merely to consider the overall unemployment rate. It's also inconsistent with what we have seen in China in recent times. (We discuss China in greater detail later in this chapter under the heading "Imported Inflation.")

Ongoing high unemployment in the United States is at least partially a reflection of the failure of the education system to deliver the skill sets that employers in today's economy need and want. The degrees we are churning out of our school system don't represent the skills and experience businesses are looking for. Engineers are a great case in point. Holding on to good engineers is becoming an increasingly costly function. Other firms want them and will poach them from competitors, because they are in relatively scarce supply. The original firm will then raise wage rates on engineers to keep them happy—and prevent them from looking elsewhere for career satisfaction. Sometimes the increase isn't directly raised labor rates but rather increased overhead costs, vacation time, or other benefits that don't directly show up in the pay packet. Businesses that experience these cost increases are prone to passing them along to their customers, especially when there aren't offsetting technological advances to compensate for the higher cost.

There will be employees who want a salary increase simply because their standard of living is slipping, likely because food, electricity, and fuel costs are rising faster than their wages. This leads to frustrated employees who want to do something about it. Smart business leaders don't want demoralized or unhappy employees; that leads to people becoming unproductive and employers having an increasingly difficult time hiring and keeping the best and the brightest. We have also seen that business leaders will dole out wage and salary increases without any commensurate offsetting improvement in productivity or responsibilities simply because they are nice, want to take care of their people, and don't want to see living standards diminish if they can help it.

Whether it be a relative shortage of a particular skill set or offsetting a decline in the standard of living for employees, wages can and will go up in an era of higher natural unemployment. Full employment used to be something we thought of as occurring at around a 4 percent unemployment rate. We are estimating based on our experiences over the past several years that the full employment rate now occurs at 6 percent unemployment. If you live in a region of the country where unemployment is pushing on 6 percent or lower, it is highly likely that wage inflation is taking root. And like kudzu, once it has taken hold, this type of inflation is difficult to eradicate. This is probably the mechanism by which we will get future systemic inflation resulting from the Federal Reserve and other central bankers keeping the monetary floodgates wide open, even as we approach a point of diminishing returns in search of the bygone target once deemed full employment.

Consider also that the Federal Reserve and other central bankers may in effect be pushing against the proverbial string. The economy is asking for a skilled and experienced worker—and those attributes don't come immediately to newly minted graduates of trade schools, let alone four-year universities. Because we have a relative lack of the right people with the skill and experience in demand, the natural economic result is that price will rise because demand exceeds supply. Price in this instance is the wage we pay workers. We see this happening already—from engineers to computer numerical control operators to welders to fabric workers—and it is only the beginning.

The insourcing trend that the United States has successfully brought about is only going to fuel this inflationary tendency. GE is building more appliances in the United States; textile producers are coming back here; higher-end furniture is being produced domestically once again. Foreign-branded automobiles are increasingly being made in the United States. The demand for skilled labor is real and it is growing.

Imported Inflation

Globalization was a major force behind the deflationary trend from the early 1980s to date. Low-cost sources for a myriad of commoditized goods drove prices down—and China was one source of those low-priced imported goods. It was a less expensive place to manufacture a lot of things because labor was so cheap, companies could ignore environmental costs, and the Chinese currency was arguably being manipulated by the government.

The process of deflation is reversed when producing the product becomes more expensive in China, or any other low-cost country, compared to what it had been. In China as well as other places, the cost of labor is rising as workers need to be enticed to move to, or remain in, urban areas. The broader cost of labor goes up when work standards and working environments improve for health and safety issues. The initial ramification of this is that the margins for producing in China will become eroded, eventually to the point where either product prices must rise or a new low-cost alternative source must be developed. The latter is not easy to do. What China managed to become in such a short period is not going to be replicated easily somewhere else—for example, Africa. Higher-priced items from China, higher transportation costs for getting the goods onshore in the U.S. and European markets, and a demand for higher quality are all ways that inflation will be imported into the United States.

Managing to Win

Businesses

As strange as it may sound to a generation who grew up in an era of deflation, there are times when a business doesn't so much strive to drive price down from vendors as much as it seeks to limit by how much prices will go up. That basic economic discipline of buying low and selling high becomes more an issue of buying *relatively* low now versus being sure of paying higher prices in the future. The price today is higher than it was a year ago, but it is lower than it will be a year from now. Because business cycles influence pricing, we must always try to time purchases based on the business cycle so that we buy low and sell high; however, this is not easy to do.

Hedging is an excellent way to protect the firm from price volatility when thinking about a raw material input into the process. Hedges have time limitations and are generally useful between a singular firm and a broader universal marketplace. What follows is how a business can use the correct escalator to protect itself from inflation.

A firm enters into a long-term contract with a customer to provide a specific intermediate or finished good. It needs price escalators to ensure that the price of the product or service grows over time. The easy solution is to create a provision saying that prices will go according to the change in the overall CPI, because this covers inflation. But it doesn't cover the *specific* type of inflation from which the firm needs protection.

Let's assume you are part of a multiyear property build out. Your contract is to pour cement—lots of it. For the year ending July 2013, the overall CPI recorded an inflation rate of 2 percent. The cement PPI the Bureau of Labor Statistics (BLS) published posted a 5.1 percent increase for the same period. You are going to need the higher price adjustment, 5.1 percent, to cover your most important cost factor: cement. It will cover your general inflation cost increases of 2 percent as well. You have just protected your margin.

The preceding demonstrated what the cement contractor would desire. If you were managing the build out and wanted to keep costs down, you would want to use the overall CPI and not the PPI. If you were up against a shrewd negotiator, you might be able to negotiate to the slightly broader construction materials PPI. The logic is right, but the price change still favors you, the acquiring entity, because the PPI was up just 2 percent year over year in our example. You can anticipate what is going to work best for you, depending on your position in the negotiation, by making yourself familiar with the PPI and CPI series that the BLS provides—and simply observing which ones are more prone to rising faster or rising slower. You want to select price indices that *maximize the appearance of inflation* when dealing with customers and select those that *minimize inflation when striking a deal with vendors.*

Besides selecting the right price escalator for contract use, firms will also benefit by replacing people with technology in their production or service process. The cost of capital is relatively fixed compared with the cost of labor during inflation periods—something that's likely to be especially true in our future environment of relatively scarce experienced labor with the skill sets we really need or want. The sooner an enterprise embarks on this strategy, the better, given that interest rates are going to rise in tandem with inflation. Leveraging up early in the inflation cycle is superior to later in the cycle, but later is better than never. Inflation favors borrowers as long as you have the means to retire the debt. You essentially pay back the strong dollars you borrowed today with cheaper, inflated dollars in the future. Besides reducing your exposure to the upward spiral of labor prices, the application of the right technologies is an effective means of achieving efficiencies that will help retard the trend of higher prices in your business process, be it for raw materials, intermediate goods, or finished goods and services. Thus, capital expenditures to drive efficiencies will help you by providing for lower-cost (pre-inflation) capital expenditures now, lower interest rates than your competitors will be forced to pay (enhancing your cash flow in comparison with theirs), easier repayment through the use of inflated dollars, and the efficiency gains that will help protect you from pervasive inflationary pressures.

Of course, some labor is necessary. In these cases, you want to nego-tiate labor contracts or agreements at the bottom of the business cycle. Lock in labor prices for three to four years; that should be sufficient to cover the duration of a typical business cycle.

You also want to combat inflationary pressures that squeeze your margins by increasing prices during phase B of the business cycle—the point at which business conditions are improving at an accelerating pace. If you compute your own rates-of-change, phase B is when your 12/12 rate-of-change is rising higher and higher above zero. Price increases are going to work best where there is product or service differentiation. It is necessary that you know what your competitive advantages are and that you communicate these differentiators very clearly. Our good friend and best-selling author Jaynie Smith has done excellent work around the world in this arena, and we recommend con-tacting her at jsmith@smartadvantage.com or getting her easy-to-read but informative book *Creating Competitive Advantage*.

Smith's core premise is that very few companies fully understand the difference between a strength and competitive advantage. Smith's company, Smart Advantage, Inc., often uncovers scores of existing competitive advantages that businesses have not previously identified and used in their sales and marketing. Therefore, price often becomes the tiebreaker when their customers make buying decisions.

Creating Competitive Advantage cautions organizations to avoid "dangerous disparity"—the difference between what a company thinks customers value and the actual reasons behind customers' buying decisions. The key question is: Are you selling traits A, B, and C, when the customer wants D, E, and F? "Be careful that you are creating competitive advantages that customers value, not what you think they 'should' value," Smith and coauthor William Flanagan warn. According to their research, which is based on customer feedback, the hierarchy of buying criteria often differs greatly from what sellers think.

Another effective strategy is to own the capital needed in the economic process. A simple example of this is own property, rather than lease it. Lease costs escalate with inflation. Your cost of capital to acquire the property need not rise. All else being equal, your cash flow improves through time, and you get the wealth-creating benefits of capital appreciation.

Individuals

It is crucial for individuals to invest in assets that tend to fare well during periods of inflation during the forthcoming inflation period. People need to understand that there are different types of inflation against which they must protect themselves and that it's dangerous to *over*estimate the inflation ahead. Underlying all these points is that the individual must make a balanced decision based on his or her unique age, risk tolerance, and goal variables. We discuss these in greater detail in Chapter 14, but for now, we will lay out some general ideas for consideration within the context of prolonged nonhyperinflation.

The smartest thing that individuals can do during a period of inflation is to borrow once, early in the scheme of things (in essence, *now*), and use that money to buy wealth-creating assets. Of course, the amount of money you should borrow is definitely an open question subject to several factors—your risk tolerance, for one thing, and how soundly you want to sleep every night. You should not be borrowing money if you are within 10 years of retirement. If the runway to retirement is longer than that, using other people's money to bankroll your inflation hedge could very well make a great deal of sense.

Keep in mind that this is an economist's approach. Most of our investment advisor friends turn a little pale at the thought of the typical individual going into debt when presented with the scenario of a Great Depression in 2030 preceded by generally modest inflation. We don't think they calculate that 2030 is 16 years from now. But you aren't typical if you are reading this book. You need to push the economic envelope by leveraging the future inflation with borrowed funds. Go for the gold and leverage now to pay the loan back in cheaper dollars in the future.

There are numerous ways to cover the inflation threat. Just keep in mind the name of the game is to have more buying power come 2030 than you have today despite inflation. Our partial list does not cover all the potential scenarios, and it certainly doesn't anticipate the new investment vehicles that will be created in the future. However, this short list is a good starting point. One thing you will note about the alternatives listed here is that although their price may go up or down based on market conditions, none of them depreciate. This may seem like a simple point, but buying a high-priced asset that is going to *depreciate* for the next 10 to 20 years is not investing in preparation for a depression that is likely to hit around 2030. No matter what the salesperson tells you, the car you are going to drive is *not* an investment—and the extra warranty you purchase is not a means of protecting that investment.

Investments to Make to Leverage Future Inflation

- Gold and other precious metals
- Farmland
- Urban real estate (single family and multifamily)
- Equities
- Treasury Inflation-Protected Securities (TIPS)
- Provide variable rate loans to others
- Art and collectibles

We don't think there is any reason to go all in on any one or two of these alternatives. Spread the risk and cover the different types of inflation. For example, TIPS are very good in an inflationary environment characterized by a rising CPI; however, they are a relatively poor choice when it comes to inflation in the form of an asset price bubble. For the latter, you are going to want the protection afforded by metals or land.

An ideal investment may be one where you go in at a fixed price today and can reasonably assume that your cash flow will improve along with inflation. For example, you buy an apartment building or a series of apartment buildings. Property taxes and utility costs are going to rise through time, but you are going to pass that through to the tenants—and then a little more on top of that. You are able to generate a positive cash flow immediately given a sufficient initial investment, maintain a positive cash flow as inflation moves rents higher, and realize a long-term gain on the asset as inflation generally drives property values higher.

An investment area we don't have on our list because we think it is going to be a very difficult place to maintain purchasing power is bond funds. Bond prices move inversely to interest rates—so as interest rates go up, bond prices go down. This means that the net asset value (NAV) on anything but extremely short-term to maturity bond funds will come under sustained downside pressure as inflation persists and interest rates rise. This is not to say that you should avoid bonds, just bond *funds*.

Earlier we offered a cautionary note about investing with the anticipation of inflation being higher than it is likely to be. If you are expecting hyperinflation and it does not develop, you may find yourself unpleasantly overweighted in gold for a day that never comes and underweighted in real estate because you expect the worst for the economy in the near term because of the nonexistent hyperinflation. It is all about balance, rational hedging, and thinking differently about between now and 2030 compared with the past 20 to 30 years.

Winners and Losers

Winning in the inflation future between now and the projected 2030–2040 depression means:

- Defining a competitive advantage and having the discipline to regularly raise prices
- Knowing how to effectively use price escalators to your advantage
- Borrowing early in the inflation process
- Locking in labor and commodity prices at business cycle lows
- Using technological advancements to continuously improve efficiencies
- Saving enough to cover the increasing cost of health care
- Investing in wealth-creating assets

Companies and individuals run the risk of setting themselves up for financial failure if they:

- Buy depreciating assets instead of wealth-creating assets
- Invest heavily in bond funds as a retirement vehicle

- Give in to the psychology of, "Buy now; it will only cost more in the future" late in the inflation trend

- Have variable-rate loans

- Use simple savings accounts and certificates of deposits as primary savings vehicles

- Rent or lease instead of own

- Think using the CPI is an effective price escalator when dealing with customers

Appendix to Chapter 5

Figure 5.6 illustrates an economic principle called the Phillips Curve. It works like this in the short run: there is a trade-off to be had between inflation and unemployment. If you are worried about unemployment and would like it to come down, don't worry about creating inflation; indeed, a little inflation seems to be a healthy choice. So, our Federal Reserve and other central bankers will grow the money supply and drop

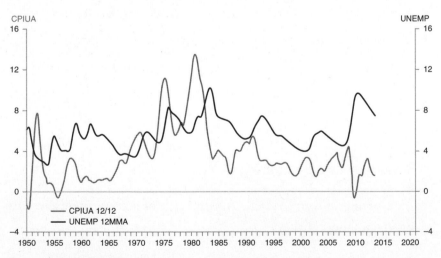

Figure 5.6   Phillips Curve
Source: ITR Economics.

interest rates in an attempt to make money cheap, encouraging consumers to buy and businesses to hire to keep up with the newly created demand.

That's the theory, of course; it doesn't always work. Notice in Figure 5.6 that after most trend lows in the CPI, the number of people unemployed continues to come down. The favorable trend in unemployment tends to continue until we approach a high in inflation. The most likely reason an inflationary trend is about to reverse from rise to decline is because monetary policy shifts from stimulative to restrictive. The money supply growth rate is reduced, interest rates are raised, and credit conditions tighten. Inflation is stopped, but so is the downward trend in unemployment because overall business conditions are deteriorating and we initially are not hiring as much as before, trending toward eventually laying off people. That is short term. There is typically an 18-month lead time between a trend reversal in the CPI and a corresponding reversal in the unemployment trend. The 18 months holds whether we focus on CPI highs or CPI lows.

6 Sovereign Debt—Harmless or Toxic?

Not Just an American Problem

National debt is on the minds of taxpayers, financiers, and government leaders across the world. World debt is currently more than $53.4 trillion at the time of this writing. The amount of debt is $17.4 trillion in the United States alone. Our work puts us in contact with people in more than three dozen countries, and we see daily how the concern regarding sovereign debt in the United States and elsewhere seems to transcend differences in culture and language. Can the world continue to add debt with economic and financial license? Strangely, some people—including some Keynesian-minded economists and government leaders—believe the answer is yes.

But these people are wrong. And their mistaken belief could lead to the suffering of millions of U.S. citizens and millions more around the world.

The financial threat is real and it is growing. Fortunately, some forward-thinking governments are meeting the problem head on and working toward real solutions. These countries, including countries such as Canada, Australia, and Mexico, will be the winners in the

2020s and beyond. Others, including the United States, are moving in the wrong direction—that is, simply continuing to incur debt. As a result, we will be experiencing the painful results of today's inability to solve the problem.

This chapter discusses both the relative winners and the absolute losers. It's critical to note that there are only *relative* winners, because the size and scope of the American problem will have a negative impact on the rest of the world's welfare as we head into the 2030s.

A Global Perspective

There are several ways to view the sovereign debt issue. The explosion of the amount of debt is behind the looming financial crisis for those countries that are unable to control their budgetary problems. See Table 6.1. The second column shows the debt in U.S. dollars (USD) to provide for easy comparison and a relative ranking as to the size of the problem. The third column exhibits the significant increases in debt in these eight nations from just 2000 to 2010.[1] The last column to the right shows debt as a percent of gross domestic product (GDP) in 2011.

Table 6.1 clearly shows the size and scope of the debt problem in the United States, Japan, and the United Kingdom. Although Germany does not look as bad on the surface, it will also face serious issues in the years to come—and we'll address Russia, Mexico, and Australia in a later section in greater detail. For now, simply note that Mexico and Australia are set to provide many more opportunities than Russia in the years to come and indeed more than many other nations as well.

The United States is a large debtor nation at more than $12.2 trillion back in 2011. The U.S. Debt Clock shows U.S. national debt at just over $17.4 trillion as of January 2014, as compared with an estimated GDP

---

[1]OECD stat extract, http://stats.oecd.org/index.aspx?queryid=8089. Debt growth from 2000 to 2010.

Table 6.1 Sovereign Debt

	2011 Debt in Trillions of USD	Percent Increase	Debt as a Percentage of GDP
United States	12.259	166.0	81.80
Japan	8.720	119.0	189.80
United Kingdom	1.534	240.0	101.20
Germany	1.442	101.0	55.60
Canada	0.869	99.0	52.50
Mexico	0.291	117.0	26.99
Russia	0.156	—	9.30
Australia	0.388	170.0	30.60

*All debt computations are based on local currencies.
Source: World Bank; Mexico data from OECD.

of $16.0 trillion. The debt increase from 2005 and the other metrics presented in Table 6.1 show that the United States has a significant problem—one we address in greater detail in Chapter 7. The focus here is on a larger global view.

The United States, the Japanese, and the UK central governments' debt levels are high, both in monetary terms and as a percent of GDP. They have continued to grow at warp speed because of the 2008–2009 Great Recession and these governments' belief that they needed to undertake massive deficit spending to keep the situation from worsening. This emergency spending came on the heels of generous entitlement programs that are under critical financial stress. Our earlier chapter on demographics illustrated that the sheer number of baby boomers worldwide will add considerable strain to global central government budgets, which will require governments' additional borrowing to meet these future entitlement-based obligations.

Germany and Canada are in better shape than the United States; the size of their debt is more manageable as compared with GDP. However, a low fertility rate in Germany ensures that existing and future taxpayers will be paying more income taxes to maintain the status quo. Japan and the United Kingdom are already in very difficult debt situations at 189.8 percent and 101.2 percent of GDP, respectively. Their negative demographic trends—combined with these debt levels—suggest very real future risk exists for Japan and the United Kingdom.

Mexico, Russia, and Australia are clearly faring better than the other economies on the list in terms of their debt load—and among these three, Mexico and Australia are better positioned than Russia. The first two have growing populations, meaning more future taxpayers. Russia's negative demographic trend will cause the country to struggle, as will its fertility rate of 1.61,[2] which ranks 178 out of 224 nations. Emigration to Russia is not enough to offset the population drain that occurs when deaths outnumber births. This leaves Russia with a future deficit of young workers and taxpayers, resulting in a financial strain on the system with future taxpayers having to bear an increasing tax bite out of their personal income. Russia may be relatively better positioned in terms of debt through the near term, but the weight of the negative demographics, in conjunction with growing energy independence in key regions around the world, strongly suggests that investments made in Russia in the 2020s could be at increasing risk.

It's also worth warning that the World Bank ranks Russia 92 out of 189 in terms of ease of doing business.[3] The country's problems center on the ability (or lack thereof) to get electricity, get construction permits, get credit, and protect investors. By comparison, the United States ranks 4; Greece, 72; China, 96; and Australia, Canada, Germany, and Japan, very well in these terms.

Australia's fertility rate of 1.77 is better than Russia's but still not enough to keep the population growing naturally. Fortunately,

---

[2]All fertility and population growth estimates come from the CIA World Factbook https://www.cia.gov/library/publications/the-world-factbook/geos/as.html.
[3]World Bank www.doingbusiness.org/rankings.

Australian immigration overcomes this deficiency, thereby allowing for population growth and thus for future workers and taxpayers.

Countries that warrant further analysis based on the debt and demographics cited previously include Canada, Mexico, and Australia. These countries' rich natural resources should provide for economic opportunities in the upcoming inflation cycle; additionally, they exhibit manageable debt levels and encouraging population trends. By extension, take a good look at most of Latin America for growth opportunities. Check for countries with growing populations, specifically in the middle class. Some, such as Chile and Peru, may be relatively small, but they will provide your company with an upside market potential or at least provide consumers for the world's goods. And that should indirectly benefit your company if you are positioned well away from the end consumer (e.g., your company makes aircraft engine parts).

Table 6.2 shows seven of the eight nations presented in Table 6.1 but in terms of the percentage of central government revenue needed just to make interest payments on existing debt. Given that the public debt is increasing daily in these countries, this percentage will only

Table 6.2   Government Revenue Needed to Make Interest Payments

	Percentage of Revenue Needed in 2011
Japan	15.68
United States	12.76
Canada	9.54
United Kingdom	8.71
Germany	5.31
Russia	1.52
Australia	5.28

Source: World Bank.

increase as the years go by—unless there are significant tax increases or spending cuts. Remember: when more revenue is required to just make interest payments, it means there is less available for entitlements or discretionary spending. This pressure will cause some nations to borrow more, and that increased borrowing increases budgetary pressures. The financial pressure will build and build until a crisis occurs, especially in those nations with a declining population. The United States and Japan will feel tremendous strain on their respective cash flows as the debt and interest rates grow. And Japan is in the unfortunate position of also having to contend with a negative demographic trend.

The United States spends 12.76 percent of its federal revenue just to pay interest on *past spending*. Nations such as China and Germany have a clear advantage over us, because a larger percentage of their central government budget is available for domestic entitlement programs (such as Medicare, prescription drug programs, Social Security, and food assistance programs), defense, or other discretionary spending items.

What's not evident from Table 6.2 is that Canada and Russia have seen a 2010 to 2011 *reduction* in the percentage of revenue needed to make interest payments, but virtually all other nations have seen an *increase*. Canada will likely continue this trend; it has a balanced budget forecasted by fiscal year 2015–2016 with a reduction of public debt likely to begin in fiscal year 2016–2017. This reduction in the cost of financing would allow Canada to enjoy a more positive financial environment, lighter tax increases on businesses and individuals in future years, and lower borrowing costs than the United States or other high-debt nations. These lower borrowing costs become a virtuous cycle that serves to accelerate its positive financial picture with each passing year. Reducing public debt and maintaining a strong national balance could have the longer-term impact of strengthening the Canadian dollar (C$) in comparison to the USD.

Of course, a stronger C$ will affect business and investment strategies. U.S.-made goods will have a cost advantage in Canada as the

USD weakens in relation to the C$; concurrently, it will be harder for Canadian firms to sell into the United States. Canadian businesses should consider opening U.S. operations as a natural hedge against a strong C$. This will keep companies competitive in the vast U.S. market and keep their brand and quality alive while taking advantage of the local U.S. currency values.

Canadian investors will have the advantage of a relatively stable and strong C$ compared with the United States, where inflationary pressures and international balance sheet pressures may reduce the U.S. dollar's value and thus purchasing power, particularly as we approach 2030. U.S. investors can potentially preserve purchasing power by investing in Canadian equities or commodity-based enterprises (e.g., companies involved in energy, mining, and lumber)—firms that should flourish in a stable financial environment and a world of inflation.

Table 6.3 compares the wealth of a nation's citizens to the debt owed by its working-age citizens (15 to 64 years old). Column C levels the playing field by comparing debt to GDP. This table conveys the fact that a nation with a high level of debt *may not be* in financial trouble—*if* it is wealthy enough to carry that debt, much like a person with a $200,000/year income can more easily afford a $170,000 mortgage (because he or she has a debt-to-income ratio of 0.85). Concurrently, a person making $60,000/year may have a hard time making the mortgage payments on a considerably smaller $90,000 mortgage (with a debt-to-income ratio of 1.5). Thus, the lower the ratio, the easier it is for the nation's people to carry the debt load—regardless of the debt or income's actual dollar size.

As we can see, China's GDP per capita is below the world's average of $12,700, and it carries $1.66 trillion in debt. But the burden per person is negligible given the size of the population. The average Chinese citizen may be poorer than the world's average, but each citizen has essentially no debt at $37 per person. Russia and Mexico's populations are able to carry the debt burden easily—for now. We've already

Table 6.3   Some Problem Nations

	A	B	C
		2011 Debt per Person	
	GDP per Capita	**Age 15 to 64,**	**Ratio of**
Country	**in USD**	**in USD**	**B to A**
United States	50,700	39,343	0.78
Canada	43,400	25,203	0.58
Australia	43,300	13,865	0.32
Germany	39,700	23,982	0.60
United Kingdom	37,500	33,256	0.89
Japan	36,900	68,223	1.85
Russia	18,000	2,083	0.12
Mexico	15,600	2,618	0.17
China	9,300	37	0.004

Source: World Bank.

mentioned the problem that will arise as Russia's population shrinks in the 2020s. Mexico's fertility rate (2.25) and population growth rate (1.07 percent/year) ensure that the nation will not be swamped by debt given current conditions. Australia and Canada are also in a good position to weather higher interest rates and any global debt storm given their relative position on the table. But Germany's negative demographics (fertility rate of 1.42 percent and population growth rate of −0.19 percent) will make the debt burden increasingly heavy on the populace in future years.

The United States and the United Kingdom clearly rank poorly in this table. Both have an elevated ratio of debt per person compared with the other nations, which makes their debt relatively unaffordable. This will make it harder for the United States, the United Kingdom, and Japan to borrow significant sums for bailout programs during the next financial crisis. It becomes especially unaffordable in the

United Kingdom and Japan given the projections of population decline between now and 2025.

We could rightfully consider Japan the worst off in terms of debt, with a level at 180.8 percent of GDP—and the fact that it has more than doubled its debt load in the first decade of this century. In addition, it takes a staggering 15.68 percent of Japan's federal revenue just to make interest payments—and the debt per person greatly exceeds the GDP per person. These facts alone should give anyone pause regarding the sustainability of Japan's national finances—a problem that its shrinking population will only exacerbate. This decline of 0.1 percent annually[4] has come because of a low fertility rate—1.39, ranking Japan at 208 out of 224 nations—as opposed to the early deaths of senior citizens. And it will mean fewer taxpayers to carry the load in each successive year.

Investors need to be aware of the long-term implications for Japan and plan accordingly for an exit strategy in the first half of the 2020s. They must be careful about making long-term investments in Japan; the economic trends are stacked up against what is currently the third-largest economy in the world. We can expect Japan's global economic standing to erode—along with the value of Japanese businesses that depend on Japan-based labor. We can also expect the yen to lose value through time for the same reasons: too much debt and a declining national income. A weaker yen will invite inflation into the economy, something that's very painful on an older population living on a fixed income. There will concurrently be more people pensioned off into expensive programs while there are fewer taxpayers to carry the burden.

The situation in the United States is not as drastic because the U.S. population is still growing. Yes, aging Americans will be expensive and will eventually provide a crushing blow to federal and state budgets, but population growth will push the problem out to about 2030. Japan's problems will come more quickly than in the United States,

---

[4]Source: World Bank.

the European Union, and China. When they do come, the United States will also feel the pain. Japan holds $1.1744 trillion in U.S. Treasuries—larger than the next five entities combined—making it the second-largest U.S. Treasuries holder. Because debt problems will prevent Japan from being able to buy U.S. debt in the 2020s, this falling away of a major debt purchaser will increase interest rates as the United States moves to attract new buyers to a risk-based commodity. The problem will become even worse when Japan is forced to sell U.S. Treasuries actively as its internal demand for the yen increases with its domestic pension needs. Higher interest rates in the United States will add to the federal budget problems, even as population aging worsens the same federal budget. More money for aging Americans, and more money for interest payments, will either drive tax rates higher—or force the U.S. government to cut spending elsewhere. Either way, economies will take a hit year after year after year until the pressures are removed—in essence, when lower interest rates come to pass or the aging population no longer receives benefits by act of law or because of death.

Summary

Australia, Canada, and Mexico are clearly the winners and are worth a long look in terms of investment opportunities and market potential. These nations are poised economically and demographically for growth from now until approximately 2030. In the next chapter, we discuss how even these healthy nations will face overwhelming economic problems as the United States moves into depression around 2030.

Businesses and investors must be especially careful regarding their exposure to Japan, the United Kingdom, Germany, and Russia as we move into the 2020s, especially in the latter half of the decade. Debt and demographic issues are likely to create an increasingly difficult environment for businesses and investors. Russia is already a difficult place to do business—and we expect the situation to deteriorate with mounting economic pressures.

The United States is carrying an enormous debt load that will become a significant factor in the coming Great Depression. The next chapter takes a closer look at the United States, the impact of rising interest rates, how this country will affect the winners presented previously, and the reliability of debt projections.

7 A Closer Look at the United States

The U.S. Problem Becomes the World's Problem

Where Are We Now?

According to the International Monetary Fund, the United States has a serious debt to gross domestic product (GDP) comparison problem. We are also a significant debtor nation compared with other populous nations. In fact, the United States is the *second-highest-ranking* debtor nation on Figure 7.1, which measures the amount of federal debt as a percentage of GDP.

Sadly, the problem is only going to get significantly worse, not better. The U.S. Congressional Budget Office (CBO), a group that uses current laws and trends to make predictions, foresees the U.S. debt level approaching Japan's by 2038. As discussed in the previous chapter, this will mean a need for more taxes, spending cuts, borrowing—or some combination of the three. Even without more borrowing, higher interest rates are going to put a lot of pressure on the federal budget. Corporate tax rates in 2013 in the United States were nominally the highest in the industrialized world.[1] We can reasonably expect that

---

[1] "Corporate Tax Rates Table," KPMG International, accessed March 8, 2014, www.kpmg.com/global/en/services/tax/tax-tools-and-resources/pages/corporate-tax-rates-table.aspx.

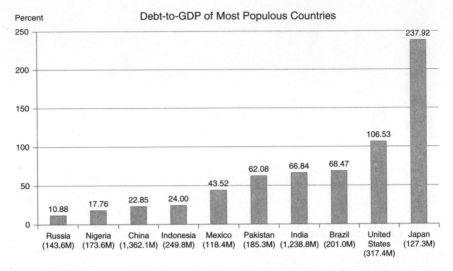

Figure 7.1   How the United States Compares to Other Nations

Data note: Data for Bangladesh (eight most populous country) unavailable.

Source: International Monetary Fund.

rising tax rates further on businesses could affect business formations and capital expenditures negatively here in the United States and keep foreign companies from moving here. Plus, as Figure 7.2 and Figure 7.3 show, the U.S. government is not particularly good at taking increased cash and using it to pay down the debt.

Figure 7.2 shows that the federal government can realize a significant increase in revenue through time and *still* create annual deficits through overspending. Notice that the projection for revenue growth picks up quite a bit between 2013 and 2017, and the budget deficit is projected to remain historically wide.

Figure 7.3 takes a different look at the situation; the federal government's total debt is shown through time, as opposed to the *annual* budget deficits shown in Figure 7.2. We can see here that federal revenues have been steadily increasing since 1940, yet the debt has been growing faster. History shows that increasing the rate of growth in revenues is

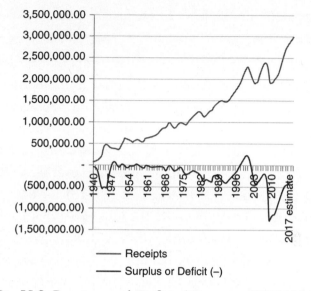

Figure 7.2 U.S. Receipts and Deficit (Constant FY2005 M$) 1940–2018

Source: White House, Office of Management and Budget.

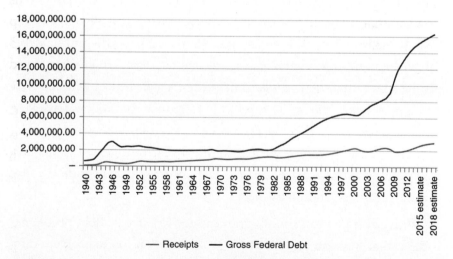

Figure 7.3 U.S. Receipts and Federal Debt (Constant FY2005 M$) 1940–2018

Source: White House, Office of Management and Budget.

not likely to result in less debt. This tells us that Congress is not good at living within its means. We can raise taxes all we want—but that doesn't mean the government will use them to reduce the public debt.

You may be wondering whether the growth in the size of the U.S. economy accounts for the revenue growth—and whether revenues are really just keeping pace with the economic growth, while expenditures are expanding in response to political promises and perceived need. The reality is that federal revenues are growing faster than the nation— something that's evidenced by the fact that federal revenues are an increasingly larger percent of GDP. The CBO is estimating that federal revenues will grow as a percentage of GDP from now through 2038. The federal government will be consuming an ever larger piece of the economic pie—but still won't be able to balance the budget or reduce the ever-growing debt load. The problem is not a lack of revenue; it is a *spending problem*.

I (Alan) took an unscientific poll of attendees from our diverse events for a period of several months in 2012. I asked if they would be willing to pay more in taxes if they were constitutionally guaranteed that the increased revenue would go toward reducing the public debt. Approximately 90 percent of the hands would go up. I then asked those people who raised their hands to raise them again if they believed that Congress would *actually use* the funds to reduce the public debt. Not one hand was ever raised in the dozens of venues where I tried this. As a country and society, we are skeptical that our elected leadership would pay down the debt. And the facts in these graphs indicate that this skepticism is wholly justified.

Why can't a nation simply print money to solve its debt problems? Indeed, that solution is often posed as *the* solution to the problem during our question and answer sessions. Although it seems simple, it is not. Massive printing of currency—because, after all, we are talking about *$17 trillion* in debt—reduces or *deflates* the value of that currency, as it would with any commodity. Remember: the U.S. dollar is not backed by gold and has no *intrinsic* value. When borrowers know a nation is creating money out of thin air, then that currency's purchasing power is likely to diminish eventually. This in turn prompts investors (lenders) to demand a higher rate of interest to offset the increased currency risk. This adverse cycle causes doubts to exacerbate the problem and accelerate the potential fiscal crisis—and brings the resulting fiscal deterioration on quite quickly.[2]

Higher interest payments negatively affect the federal budget—and the CBO expects interest rates to rebound from 2013's unusually low levels in the coming years. This could result in a sharp increase in the government's cost of borrowing. The CBO estimates that interest payments on the public debt will grow from 1.9 percent of GDP in 2013 to 4.9 percent of GDP in 2038.[3] This might not sound like much, but 4.9 percent is what we are currently paying for Social Security as a percent of GDP. Social Security consumes 22 percent of the federal budget.[4]

In addition, a decline in the value of the U.S. dollar in the global marketplace would make imported goods more expensive. Inflation is a drag on economic growth, hurts lower-income wage earners and people on fixed incomes, and leads to higher interest rates on commercial and personal loans, all of which are factors that lead people to spend less and eventually provoke recession. And if the inflation and resulting interest rate rise are steep enough—and accompanied by other significant factors, such as the demographic trends presented earlier in this book—the result can be an economic depression.

---

[2]David Greenlaw, James D. Hamilton, Peter Hooper, and Frederic S. Mishkin, "Crunch Time: Fiscal Crises and the Role of Monetary Policy" (paper presented at the U.S. Monetary Policy Forum, New York City, February 22, 2013).
[3]Congressional Budget Office, *The 2013 Long-Term Budget Outlook*, last modified October 31, 2013, https://cbo.gov/publication/44521.
[4]"Policy Basics: Where Do Our Federal Tax Dollars Go?" Center on Budget and Policy Priorities, last modified April 12, 2013, www.cbpp.org/cms/index .cfm?fa=view&id=1258.

We are currently able to handle our debt payments, thanks to record-low interest rates on 10-year Treasury Notes courtesy of former Fed Chairman Dr. Bernanke. However, that will not last, and there will be a massive amount of interest to pay on a mountain of debt. And it's not a problem we can print our way out of.

Where Are We Going?

The CBO estimates for public debt as a percent of GDP in the United States are shown on Figure 7.4. This destructive scenario will continue until we first have a balanced budget and then run a surplus that we can use to reduce the debt burden.

Of course, not everyone believes the United States needs a balanced budget or that we can ever reach that goal.[5] The preceding discussion on the cost of interest payments alone makes it plain that we cannot continue on the current path—given the financial risk of a weakened balance sheet, the exposure to foreign creditors, and the exploding demographically based costs in the 2030s. There are no reasonable estimates of when the United States will balance the budget and begin to reduce the debt burden. The CBO estimates that the problem will continue to grow as we move toward 2038.

It may look like just a bump on the graph, but *The 2013 Long-Term Budget Outlook* by the CBO states that:

> Between 2009 and 2012, the federal government recorded the largest budget deficits relative to the size of the economy since 1946, causing federal debt to soar. Federal debt held by the public is now about 73 percent of the economy's annual output, or gross domestic product (GDP). That

---

[5]Lisa Desjardins, "Why the U.S. May Never Have a Balanced Budget Again," CNN.com, March 29, 2012, www.cnn.com/2012/03/29/politics/balanced-budget.

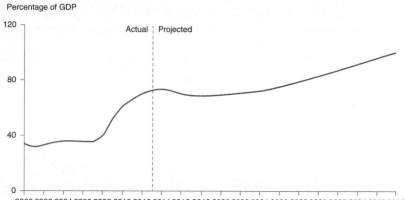

Figure 7.4 Federal Debt Held by the Public under CBO's Extended Baseline

Source: Congressional Budget Office, September 2013, www.cbo.gov/publication/44521.

percentage is higher than at any point in U.S. history except a brief period around World War II, and it is twice the percentage at the end of 2007. If current laws generally remained in place, federal debt held by the public would decline slightly relative to GDP over the next several years, the Congressional Budget Office (CBO) projects. After that, however, growing deficits would ultimately push debt back above its current high level. CBO projects that federal debt held by the public would reach 100 percent of GDP in 2038, 25 years from now, *even without accounting for the harmful effects that growing debt would have on the economy* (emphasis added).... Moreover, debt would be on an upward path relative to the size of the economy, *a trend that could not be sustained indefinitely* (emphasis added).[6]

---

[6]Congressional Budget Office, *Long-Term Budget Outlook*, 1.

We are clearly anticipating some financial troubles in the 2030s—and the CBO knows it.

We are heading into a future where federal government spending will continue to expand in relation to the economy; specifically, the CBO projects an increase to 26 percent of GDP. By way of comparison, the federal government comprised 22 percent of U.S. GDP in 2012, with the average for the past 40 years being 20.5 percent. That increase will come because of the rising costs of existing health care programs, the implementation of the Affordable Health Care Act, and the increased demands upon the Social Security Administration. It is estimated that health care and Social Security will someday comprise 14 percent of GDP, up from the 40-year average of 7 percent. And, of course, that money must come from somewhere. The CBO estimates that revenues will only reach 19.5 percent of GDP in 2038 while spending reaches 26 percent (the 40-year average is 17.5 percent).

So what does this mean for you? Readers should plan for either a major transfer of wealth from the private sector into the public sector through taxation or massive increases in borrowing. In either case, it bodes ill for the business sector.

Figure 7.5 presents a summary of how the U.S. government is driving the future. The cost of health care and net interest payments will climb through 2038, which will effectively squeeze out other noninterest spending from now through the forecast horizon. Your favorite government program and other nonmandatory government agencies will find it harder and harder to get funding. Last, the Social Security line levels off in the 2030s because of the increasing number of baby boomers' deaths in that decade. Even then, the bite out of the budget is larger than it is today.

The official estimate from the CBO calls for a dramatic increase between now and 2023. See Table 7.1.

Many people wonder how we can afford these programs *now*. Imagine how much more financial pressure there will be on the government just nine years from now.

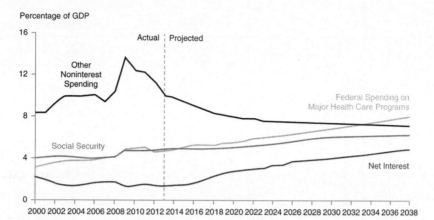

Figure 7.5 Components of Total Spending under CBO's Extended Baseline

Source: Congressional Budget Office, September 2013,
www.cbo.gov/publication/44521.

Table 7.1 Troubles Ahead

	2014	**2023**	**Percent Increase**
Social Security	$854b	$1,423b	66.3 percent
Health Care Programs	$951b	$1,843b	93.8 percent

Source: Congressional Budget Office.

State and Local Governments

The problem of increasing debt levels is not limited to the U.S. government. State and local governments have accumulated approximately $3.2 trillion in their own debt, with unfunded retirement obligations at about another $3 trillion. The rate of rise since 2000 is staggering, as shown in Figure 7.6. We can see how the massive run-up in debt since 2000 pretty much took place in years of economic growth and *not* because of the Great Recession's cash crunch. All 50 individual states would have to run a combined budget surplus of $150 billion a year for 20 years to pay off that debt before 2030. Instead, the states had a

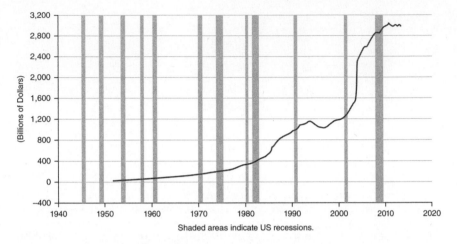

Figure 7.6   State and Local Debt—without Including Retirement Funds

Source: Federal Reserve Bank of St. Louis, 2014 researchstlouisfed.org.

combined revenue shortfall of $64 billion in 2012. Results were better in 2013 with at least half the states reporting a *surplus*. However, it is unlikely that states will use the surplus to pay down their debt levels. Indeed, while newspaper articles portend some saving for a raining day, governors on both sides of the aisle are talking about increased spending—*not* debt reduction. Carrying the debt into the future in this way will put a strain on state budgets.

According to the U.S. Census Bureau, the 50 states combined paid approximately $49.9 million in interest payments in 2012, which comes to about 2.52 percent of their total expenditures. The average interest rate on state debt in 2012 was 1.733 percent and edged even lower in 2013.

The problem is that interest rates are going to move higher, not lower, in the future—because growing rates are consistent with our forecast of inflation in coming years. This trend will have a significant adverse impact on state budgets, as shown on Table 7.2.

Table 7.2 Budget Pressure: States

	Projected Interest Rate	Interest Expense on $3.2 Trillion	Amount Increase from 2012
2018	5 percent	$160 million	$110.0 million
2023	7 percent	$224 million	$174.1 million
2028	9 percent	$288 million	$238.1 million

Source: U.S. Census Bureau.

Higher interest payments at the state level, along with the demographic cost demands, will push the states to increase taxes, cut spending, or employ some combination of the two. It's the same situation the federal government will face—only states do not have the option to print money. Individuals and businesses in debt-ridden states should expect an increased state burden on their income.

Spreading the Pain around the World

Many people assume China is the same size as the United States, but, in fact, the U.S. economy is almost twice as large (89.7 percent larger to be exact). What happens in the United States therefore has a large impact on China and other nations in terms of trade, given that all the nations included in this book depend on trade as significant contributors to their GDP. Table 7.3 shows the nations we have discussed that are important trading partners to the United States—and that thus depend on a healthy U.S. economy. The figures also show that each of these countries took a significant economic hit in 2009 because of the Great Recession, which had its epicenter in the United States.

The countries cited in Table 7.3 experienced a total of 7.8 million workers displaced in 2009 alone, whereas the United States saw the unemployment ranks swell by 3.7 million. 11.5 million workers lost their jobs in that *one year*. The impact of the coming Great Depression will be significantly worse, as will be the associated strain

Table 7.3   Dependence on the United States

Country	Export as a Percent of GDP	Rank as a Source of Imports into the United States	2009 Change in GDP
Australia	21.3 percent	7	+0.2 percent
Canada	29.7 percent	3	−3.0 percent
China	27.3 percent	1	+9.0 percent
Germany	51.8 percent	6	−5.0 percent
European Union 28	43.1 percent	2	−5.8 percent
Mexico	32.9 percent	4	−5.0 percent
Russia	29.4 percent	17	−8.0 percent
United States			−2.8 percent

Source: World Bank.

on governments worldwide to provide unemployment and other benefits through an elongated economic contraction. As discussed in prior chapters, the United States is not the only nation facing a demographic problem in terms of an aging population. However, count on the United States to export its additional debt and budget problems in the same way it exported its financial problems in 2008 and 2009.

Australia fares the best of all the countries on this list, as it is less dependent on the United States in comparison with all the other nations, except for Russia. Australia's GDP edged higher in 2009, but the others' (except China's) experienced significant contractions. Its relatively small population and comparatively lighter dependence on exports will enable Australia to weather the coming economic storm better than the other nations will. You may remember that Australia also scored very well in the areas of debt and demographics.

China would appear to offer the same haven in 2030 as it seems to have done in 2009. But China's demographic problems are large, and its exports to the United States did in fact drop in 2009. The reported

9 percent growth in GDP in 2009 was largely because of stimulus spending on one-time infrastructure projects (roads, building, and rail) as opposed to being the result of solid long-term, trade-based, middle-class growth. The fact that China needed to engage in large-scale stimulus spending demonstrates its dependence on a healthy U.S. economy. Be very careful of China in the 2030s; it is poised for a significant downturn along with the United States.

Summary

The future debt level in the United States is going to have a large impact on the United States and the world. Increased borrowing costs will necessitate higher taxes, reduced government spending, or most likely a combination of the two. Readers should anticipate higher business and personal income taxes as we move closer to 2030. Tax accountants and tax lawyers should have thriving practices in the years to come.

There is another cost to the debt explosion and higher interest rates. Governments will find a dramatically reduced ability to spend money the next time there is a crisis. Austerity now would be unpleasant, but it would be a preferable alternative to the financial calamity to come.

8 Business Growth Strategies and Tactics from Now through 2029

Change is coming—it always is. Business growth strategies and tactics for the run-up to the coming Great Depression include:

- See the future before it shows up on your income statement.
- Know how to play offense and defense.
- Understand that the rules are changing.

This book is about seeing the future in broad terms so that we can all prosper professionally and personally. Looking for the trends we describe to develop and anticipating how you are going to interact with those trends is part of a successful forward-looking strategy. But there is no use having a successful long-term strategy if you don't have some complementary tactics to work through the myriad of month-to-month, year-to-year, and cycle-to-cycle twists and turns that are going to define the short term reality as we progress through the long term. It comes down to a process of metrics and making decisions based on those metrics. Our favored means of measuring business activity are monthly data, moving totals, and rates-of-change. Our first book, *Make Your Move*, does a good job of explaining how to develop and read these metrics, so we are only going to summarize that process in this book.

Monthly Moving Totals (MMTs)

Moving totals are the sum of the monthly total data for a stated number of months. For example, the 3MMT for November would be the sum of the September, October, and November monthly data. When December data become available, September is dropped from the calculation and December added. By doing so, the December 3MMT consists of the activity recorded in October, November, and December. The 12MMT is the sum of the past 12 months of data, calculated on a moving basis based on new monthly data becoming available.

Calculating Rate-of-Change

A rate-of-change figure is the ratio (the simple percentage) of a number in a data series to a preceding number in that data series. When calculating the rates-of-change, the time interval between the numbers being compared is fixed. A rate-of-change figure can tell you instantly whether activity is running below or above this time last year and by how much.

When rates-of-change move consecutively in the same direction, it indicates that activity levels are getting *progressively* better or worse compared with last year. The rate-of-change of a data series illustrates and measures *cyclical* change and identifies *trends*. The 12/12 rate-of-change is also vital to finding important relationships with leading indicators that will enable you to see down into that mine shaft to the gold below.

When calculating the 12/12 rate-of-change, the upper 12 (numerator) of the 12/12 specifies that a 12MMT comparison is being made. The lower 12 (denominator) signifies that the time interval is 12 months.

Use the Metrics

When it comes to seeing economic change before it shows up on your income statement, be sure to:

- *Set up a system of leading indicators.* Find the indicators that apply to your business, and use them to forecast future changes. Include those that we describe later in this chapter, and add any others that you have used or that might help.

- *When two of your leading indicators go up or down, pay attention.* Take notice and look to see whether other leading indicators confirm that a change in direction is real. At ITR Economics, we calculate the probabilities that trends will reverse using shortcuts that we discuss later in this book. When two of your leading indicators tell you that the wind has begun to shift, start planning because planning takes time. Decide which sails to set and who will be manning the ropes.

- *When five leading indicators reverse direction, act.* It's usually solid evidence that the economy is turning. Move forward with confidence because the system is telling you that a fundamental shift in the momentum of the economy is taking place. When five leading indicators move in the same way, it's rarely a coincidence. Each indicator that signals a reversal confirms the other indicators and verifies that the economy will shift in a new direction. When five leading indicators agree, have your resources lined up, and be ready to implement your plan because change is on the way. Many people will feel their adrenaline pumping because economic conditions are about to get exciting again!

- *Start making the tactical changes needed to implement your strategic plan.* If it turns out that the shift in the leading indicators is misleading or incomplete, you will not have overreacted. You will have simply flexed the corporate muscles you will need when the change in the business cycle has been either internally or externally verified.

We use a number of leading indicators when devising a macro-economic leading indicator system. Following are some of the major indicators we use.

1. *Corporate bond prices* (12/12 rate-of-change): Tracking the movement in corporate bond prices is an outstanding leading indicator that many forecasters overlook. We've been using it for a long time and find it extremely valuable.

   If you've heard us speak, you know that tracking corporate bond prices is one of our favorite leading indicators. We love its accuracy and prize its objectivity. The corporate bond prices 12/12 rate of change has worked extremely well no matter which political party was in control of the White House or Congress. It's been accurate in times of war or peace, inflation, deflation, changes in the Federal Reserve Board leadership, and the increased globalization of the past 30 years. Even the introduction of disco in the 1970s didn't disrupt the value of the corporate bond prices 12/12 as a leading indicator!

   How it works: If the prices for bonds that are selling through the exchanges are rising, it means that bond yields are going down, which is good for corporations because their cost of borrowing money will be less. That shows that corporate leadership is not afraid of inflation, and the lower interest rates make it easier to invest in new capital equipment and new enterprises. Remember:

   ◆ High interest rates discourage borrowing money.

   ◆ Low interest rates encourage the use of credit.

   So we want to see rising corporate bond prices because it means that more businesses can borrow money and use it to build their businesses and revenues. Corporate bond prices are one of the earliest leading indicators. Although changing corporate bond prices is the first sign of a trend the vast majority of the time, few people know that they should track them.

Lead time: Changes in corporate bond prices indicate that adjustments in the overall economy will usually occur in approximately 10 months. We advise clients that they have four quarters' lead time.

Sources: Information on corporate bond prices can be obtained from Moody's Investor Service (www.moodys.com), Bloomberg (www.bloomberg.com), and other financial services. Every month, look at the average yield for double-A-rated or triple-A-rated corporate bonds.

2. *ITR Leading Indicator:* This important indicator was developed by Brian in the late 1980s and has recently been modified by Andrew Duguay, senior economist at ITR Economics. It's a composite index that we've put together to strike a balance between two parts of our economy: consumer and industrial behavior.

How it works: The ITR Leading Indicator shows whether business-to-business activity and business-to-consumer activity are going up or going down. It contains items, financial indicators, and broader elements of economic activity that are cyclical.

Lead time: Highs are a median of 10 months. The median lead time for lows is also 10 months, with a range of 9 to 12 months.

Sources: This particular leading indicator is proprietary to ITR Economics and can be found via a subscription to the *ITR Trends Report* or *ITR Advisor.* Information on how to subscribe is at www.itreconomics.com.

3. *Institute for Supply Management's (ISM) Purchasing Managers Index:* This is a top-notch leading indicator. It takes a different slant from tracking corporate bond prices, which looks at corporate finances, and the ITR Leading Indicator, which examines a mixture of

business activities. The Purchasing Managers Index is based on a compilation of statistics based on surveys of purchasing managers. The Purchasing Managers Index is best suited for following the business-to-business side of our economy.

How it works: This index provides a good composite from the order side of business. It gathers information from purchasing managers and examines whether inventories, prices, order activity, exports, and imports are going up or down and whether delivery times are accelerating or slowing.

The ISM has done an excellent job of weighting this index, so it consistently leads the economy through highs and lows. It provides a good indication of the overall temperature of the business community.

Lead time: The typical lead time is about seven months through lows and five months through highs before a similar change will be seen in the economy as measured by U.S. industrial production.

Sources: This information can be found on the front page of any newspaper business section or at the ISM's website, www.ism.ws.

4. *U.S. Leading Indicator:* Originally compiled by the government, this is now put together and issued by the Conference Board, a private concern. It's a good indicator that is heavily weighted toward the consumer side of the economy.

How it works: Among other items, the U.S. Leading Indicator tracks the number of building permits issued. Other indicators are money supply, stock market, spread in interest rates, building permits, manufacturers' new orders for nondefense capital goods, manufacturers' new orders for consumer goods and materials, average weekly manufacturing hours, index of consumer expectations, index of supplier deliveries (vendor performance), and state initial claims for unemployment insurance.

Lead time: The typical lead time at highs is 13 months and 10 months at lows.

Source: The Conference Board issues the U.S. Leading Indicator via press releases. It is also reported in newspapers and can be accessed at www.conference-board.org.

5. *Orders vs. Inventory Levels.* This tracks both the number of orders for products and the level of company inventories. The ratio is calculated by ITR Economics using government data.

How it works: When orders are increasing and inventories are declining, it's a good indication that the economy is growing stronger. If orders are going down and inventories are growing, it indicates that we are getting into a recession. We use a ratio of inventory to orders to calculate this information.

Lead time: 11 months through highs and seven months on the median.

Source: The U.S. Department of Commerce distributes figures on new orders and inventories in its Manufacturers' Shipments, Inventories, and Orders survey. ITR Economics calculates and presents this ratio when applicable as part of our leading indicator series at company and trade association presentations.

6. *Stock market (S&P 500):* The stock market is not one of our favorite forecasting indicators, but we look at it because so many others like it. We also like to try to figure out where the stock market is heading.

How it works: When stocks rise, most consider the economy to be moving in a positive direction, and the opposite holds true when the stock market declines. The problem with the stock market as a forecasting indicator is twofold: (1) movement in the market can be coincidental, and (2) at times, the market has lagged behind the bulk of the economy. We've seen times when the stock market didn't peak until after a recession began.

On the other hand, the stock market generally reflects how well corporations are perceived to be doing. It also tracks a broad cross section of the economy and is extremely popular, so we give it consideration.

Lead time: Four months.

Warning: Many people rely on various stock market indexes to gauge the future economic climate, and others rely on one index exclusively. However, these indexes don't give the full economic picture and are not particularly reliable leading indicators.

The stock market can be useful as a part of the total picture, but it is not reliable enough to stand on its own. To compound the problem, many people constantly check the Dow Jones, S&P 500, and other indexes. They check them every day and frequently during each day, which can give them a false indication and confusing statistical noise that does not forecast real trends.

Sources: All major city and financial newspapers and online financial websites.

7. *Housing starts:* The change in the number of housing starts is a solid indicator that people can track easily. Because housing is such a huge part of the economy, the number of housing starts must be included in any leading indicator system for that system's projections to be accurate.

How it works: The number of houses started is collected, and the larger the number the more beneficial impact it has on the economy. As we've mentioned, even though a business has nothing to do with housing, the number of housing starts can affect it because it ripples through the rest of the economy. Until the housing market starts showing some improvement, it's hard to say that recovery is at hand. Until housing starts to pick up, the economy will continue to go through a lot of pain.

Lead time: During highs, housing will lead industrial production by a median of eight months. For lows, the median is six months.

Sources: The U.S. Census Bureau is a readily available source for information on housing starts. The statistics for housing starts are available by region, so people can focus on the situation in their particular area. In some states, the statistics are also available by counties.

8. *Retail sales:* The rate-of-change in retail sales is an extremely important indicator, although it doesn't provide much actual lead time regarding changes in the bulk of the economy. During good times, retail sales account for approximately 67 percent of the U.S. economy.

   How it works: When retail sales are down, the economy will not improve until consumers get back in the game. In trying to forecast change, retail sales are the last piece of the pie that must fall into place for you to know that a trend is real. When retail sales activity increases, you can feel very confident about the recovery and know that a new trend will soon take place.

   Lead time: Retail sales have a relatively short lead time through both highs and lows of two and three months, respectively, to U.S. industrial production.

   Source: U.S. Government Census Bureau.

● ● ●

Obviously, this is all going to work best if you have a working knowledge of how your specific company or market(s) relates to the general economy and to this system of leading indicators. When taking the analysis to the company level, we will find more focused, finite, related data series that routinely bring the number of indicators in the ITR Economics system to at least a dozen.

9 Offense and Defense

Strategies for the Upside of the Business Cycle

Offense and Defense

Knowing how to play offense and defense means that you can see business cycle rising trends before they occur—and can therefore get aggressive with your plans, pricing, and budgets (offense). You'll also be able to catch the weak spots of business cycle declining trends and protect your profitability, even though the economy will be going through leaner times (defense).

The business cycle consists of four Phases: A, B, C, and D.

During Phase A, the business cycle is advancing, the economy's momentum is on the upswing, and data that showed that the economy had been in recession is starting to turn in a positive direction. Figure 9.1 illustrates Phase A.

Companies can rely on two historically verifiable measures to spot this change and be confident that the business cycle is *actually* improving:

1. The majority of the leading indicators in the system that the company depends upon are moving up; and
2. The company's 12/12 rate-of-change, which measures the business's growth for 12 consecutive months, is rising.

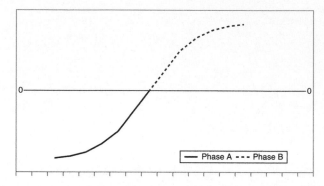

Figure 9.1   Phase A: 12/12 Rate-of-Change Is Rising toward the
Zero Line
Source: ITR Economics.

Conflicting Messages

Early Phase A can be a confusing time. Although the economy shows
encouraging signs, most decision makers are still pessimistic, fearful,
and uncertain. Because the economy has been in the dumps, an overall sense of despondency still prevails. Most of the news, analysis, and
scuttlebutt remain negative, and no one is sure *when* the economy will
improve. At this time, even optimists become guarded; the old adage,
"It's always darkest before the dawn" seems to have been coined for
these times.

Many business leaders are afraid to act when they start seeing signs
that the business cycle may be advancing toward recovery, because the
world around them is still so pessimistic. The idea of taking aggressive
action goes against their instincts and seems out of step with everyone
else. Although these executives see optimistic signs when they look at
the instruments on the dashboard—the leading indicators and 12/12
rate-of-change—they see something else when they gaze out the win-
dow: the dense fog of doom and gloom. As a result, leadership can be
reluctant to move forward at this time.

As companies advance further in Phase A, the mood slowly changes internally from uncertainty to hope. A more positive and hopeful atmosphere guardedly emerges, and people eventually begin to generally accept that the recovery is at hand. At that point, companies' competitors begin to make plans so that they can cash in on the good times that everyone agrees are in store.

Don't Delay

You will have at least a six-month jump on your competition if you act early in Phase A. By the time your competitors finally start to plan, your plans will already be in place—and you will have started implementing them.

Don't wait until you are in Phase A to position yourself to take advantage of the upturn; if you do, it will be too late. Instead, watch the signals to see when Phase A is coming, gather your resources, and plan. Then when it actually comes, you will know exactly what to do and can implement those plans.

As you move into Phase A:

- *Be entrepreneurial.* Entrepreneurs work smartly and creatively. They also work hard and don't let others tell them what they can't do. They set goals and reach them.

- *Move quickly and decisively.* Because Phase A is a time of change, opportunity, and growth, take a can-do attitude. Even though the market is soft, find ways to use its sluggishness to your advantage.

- *Don't be self-limiting.* Look for opportunities everywhere; don't say, "That's not our market." Instead, ask, "How can I get *into* that market?" Don't state, "We don't have the right person." Instead, declare, "Let's go out and get the right person."

Phase A Management Objectives

As the economy advances toward recovery, you can capitalize on the upswing by implementing the following steps that apply to your business:

Costs and Savings

1. *Negotiate union contracts.* Because the workforce has recently experienced wide layoffs, labor leaders will be less concerned about the future than they are about the here and now. They usually won't push you as hard for raises and benefits; they're just glad that their people have jobs. Phase A presents a golden opportunity for businesses to negotiate labor contracts and lock in lower labor costs for the next few years.

2. *Enter into leases.* Negotiate or renegotiate long-term leases on your fleet, machinery, and *especially* real estate. Property managers and owners cringe when we make this recommendation, but they know it makes sense. Because of the recent downturn, people who own land are now concerned about their vacancy rates; therefore, many will be willing to enter into win-win leases with potential or existing tenants. Property owners may make concessions on the rent and help tenants reduce their immediate cash flow needs in exchange for longer-term leases or paybacks at the end of lease terms. They may be more creative, especially in accepting deferrals to help their tenants survive.

3. *Lock in commodity prices.* Generally, commodity prices are a lagging economic indicator, so as your business picks up and your future starts looking brighter, enter into long-term raw material contracts before the prices escalate. Making this commitment will take courage, but down the road, the fact that you locked in long-term supply contracts at today's low prices will save you a bundle.

Build the Foundation for Recovery

4. *Make acquisitions.* The mood is gloomy during a downturn. Company owners are tired and discouraged from trying to keep their businesses afloat—especially when their profits are down and they are short on cash. They may have a fundamentally healthy business, but a fundamentally bad attitude, and therefore question whether their efforts or their company is worth the uphill battle they face. Use the prevailing pessimism to your advantage. If you make them an offer, they just may accept—and you can make a fabulous deal.

5. *Discover customer needs.* Identify which customer needs you *don't* currently serve, and determine exactly what you would need to do to fulfill those needs. Conduct customer research to discover what they're seeking, and be aware of the changing world. Introduce new product lines based on what you uncover. For instance, the younger generation of purchasers wants value and profits that are consistent with its vibrant social consciousness, so energy efficiency and green products are the new way to go. Offer products and services that focus on what customers want *now,* instead of operating as you always did in the past. Early Phase A is a great time to adjust your methods because you probably can devote the time and the talent to pursuing new approaches.

People and Leadership

6. *Implement training programs.* Because business is on the ascent, it's vital that you have enough trained employees available when demand hits its peak. Anticipate the number of orders that might stream in and how many well-trained people you will need to handle them. Then hire and train these new employees so that you will be ready for the rush. If you don't, your customer service will suffer, you will alienate customers—and they may turn to other sources. If customers leave because of poor or lack of service, it's nearly impossible to get them back.

7. *Hire top people.* Even the best employees lose their jobs during economic slumps. Lots of good people will still be out of work in Phase A or working for companies that have no vision, strategy, and direction or are on the ropes. Many of these people will be looking for other employment opportunities. This makes Phase A an ideal time to hire. If you wait until Phase B (the *really* good times), those people will probably be gone.

Growth and Expansion

8. *Invest in technology and software to improve your efficiency.* As the business cycle ascends, the cost of technology will be much lower than the cost of hiring more people. Investing in technology today will also be less expensive than it will be a year or two from now. If you can supplant people with technology, do so!

9. *Add sales staff.* Most companies wait until a growth trend is well established to hire and train new salespeople. This is usually too late—because companies tell us that it takes nine to 12 months to train new staff members. Phase A lasts about 12 months, so businesses should be hiring and training new salespeople at the bottom of Phase A so that they're good to go when they move into Phase B. Hire enough people to handle the increased loads you project; don't be caught short. Have your new sales force knock on doors that your company never approached before. The world will have changed since the last time you were gearing up for Phase B, so don't assume that you will have the same markets and customers.

10. *Place capital equipment orders.* Buying capital equipment in Phase A will be far cheaper than it will be later in Phase B. In Phase A, a great deal of both new and used equipment will be available at attractive prices, and you will have more choices as to what you can buy. The lead times will also be shorter at this phase of the business cycle than they will be down the road.

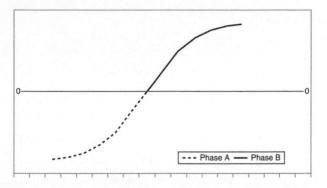

Figure 9.2   Phase B: 12/12 Rate-of-Change Is Rising Above
the Zero Line
Source: ITR Economics.

Let the Good Times Roll

The second phase of the business cycle is Phase B—a great time in the
cycle. You'll know you've made it there when your 12/12 rate-of-change
is ascending above the zero line (see Figure 9.2). Sales are running progressively higher than they did this time last year, and revenues are
climbing to the steepest portion of the rising trend.

Figure 9.2 shows Phase B of the business cycle when the 12/12
rate-of-change is rising higher and higher away from zero.

In many ways, Phase B is the best portion of the business cycle
and is usually the most exciting and exhilarating time. You get up in
the morning eager to get to work because everything is fun, alive, and
captivating. Although managing this growth could create added stress
in the latter half of Phase B, it's exciting to see the business grow and
enjoy such success.

Regardless of how good you feel during Phase B, continue to look
both ways and follow the signals before venturing out. To prolong the
time you spend in Phase B and continue enjoying the momentum,
productivity, and profits of this period, follow some of our Phase B
Management Objectives:

Open Up the Throttle

1. *Check your processes flow for potential bottlenecks.* Sure, you can handle the workload now—but can you manage it if the volume picks up another 5 percent, 10 percent, or 20 percent? Answer those questions now; work through different scenarios to look for possible bottlenecks and determine how your systems will perform when new business pours in—as it will in Phase B. Making changes *now* will be a lot easier, and probably much cheaper, than fixing breakdowns that occur when your volume has increased.

2. *Increase prices.* We touched on this earlier, but let's take it a step further. Let's assume you are busy, really busy. Your goods or services are in great demand, and you're enjoying a nice return on your investment. But you notice as more business comes in that your people are feeling increased stress, and your costs are going up because of mistakes, absences, increased inefficiencies, and overtime. Now is the perfect time to raise your prices. At first, your activity may level off; however, your profits will increase, and you can deal with your cost problems in a sane, contemplative manner.

3. *Maintain and pursue quality.* Quality counts can give you a huge competitive advantage. Most companies don't want their quality to drop, but it does—too frequently. Complacency can set in while you're focused on pursuing growth and diminish your products' or services' quality. Tie the constant need for top quality to Management Objective number 6, using your cash flow to improve company governance and make it a top ongoing priority.

    When it seems like the entire world is craving your goods or services, it can be hard to maintain your quality. However, letting it drop even the slightest amount can kill your reputation and all your years of hard, top-notch work. Commit to providing the highest quality goods and services continuously. It's what customers want and deserve. It's also a great long-term formula for beating the business cycle.

4. *Outsource.* Consider using outside manufacturing sources or sub-contracting work when internal pressures start becoming tight. It's natural to want to expand internal capacity when the future looks bright and you identify long-term needs. The tendency is to add brick, mortar, and people, thereby increasing your fixed costs and semifixed costs. Adding to your in-house capabilities, and therefore your costs, works best in these situations:

   a. You are entering a market in a new geographical area or offering a new product or service.

   b. You have an extremely long building or buying time that requires you to look beyond business cycles.

   c. You have a highly technical service or product to protect.

Look Beyond The Current Trend

5. *Ask, "What next?"* Your answers to this question will help you identify how you want your business to develop, create an overall plan, and identify the steps that will lead you to that destination. When you know what's next, you prolong your Phase B prosperity and shorten the next stage—Phase C. Your answers can also help you avoid painful Phase D altogether.

   Figuring out what's next can be difficult. Start by reviewing your objectives and what you want. For example, we all want to grow our revenues continuously, even in deteriorating or adverse economic conditions. Answering the following questions will help you decide what's next:

   a. What do I want to be two to five years from now? Do I want to be the non-executive chief executive officer with an active company president who takes care of daily operations?

   b. What do I want my company to be like in the future?

   c. Will my company develop a comprehensive, scalable market strategy?

   d. What new services and products will my customers require next year or a few years thereafter?

e. What will my customers need that they don't even know about yet?

f. Can I anticipate my customers' needs and fulfill them before my competitors are aware of those needs?

g. Do export opportunities exist that I have yet to consider?

6. *Begin missionary efforts into new markets.* Look in new and different areas. You can obtain some direction by determining what's next—identifying new geographic markets (domestic or international) or fresh services or products that will create a new market that you can offer to your existing customers or to a new group of customers within your reach. Use your cash and governance to grow in *new directions,* not just to expand your present business.

7. *Penetrate selected new accounts.* Look for potential customers in countercyclical or in acyclic industries—which include the medical, climate change, and green industries. We cover these in greater detail in Chapter 11.

8. *Stay realistic.* Beware of straight-line or linear budgets, because they often cause gross misallocations of resources with resultant profit losses. When resources are misused, publicly traded companies and their management take big hits from Wall Street.

   Business leaders have the responsibility to be good stewards of their resources, and performing rate-of-change analysis can help. Linear budgeting is essentially straight-line thinking. It's not always helpful in unusual situations; it can thwart creativity and flexibility and can generate straight-line forecasting. Throw in a healthy dose of the *not me* syndrome, and you have a prescription for disaster.

9. *Freeze your expansion plans.* Don't expand unless the expansion is related to your answer to Management Objective 5, "What's next?" We can't overemphasize the importance of this Management Objective. The optimism and euphoria of Phase B lead many decision makers to move into expansion mode when they

approach the top of this business cycle phase. We've all seen firms that take on huge expansion projects only to sell them off a few years later when they need cash.

Follow the old axiom: buy low (in the business cycle) and sell high! You don't want to expand at the top, when everything costs you more. So expand in Phase A or early Phase B, when your costs are less.

10. *Spin off weak operations.* Look at your operation, evaluate all segments, and put the weak units up for sale. Spin off segments that are only marginally profitable even in good times or that have a long cyclical decline ahead of them.

Don't be sentimental. Get rid of weak segments, even though they may have been the core of the business or near and dear to the founders or senior management.

Summary

There are lots of positive actions to take while the economy is expanding, and more important, while your business is picking up momentum. The whole environment is conducive to favorable outcomes, and every action seems to be a step forward. It is a great time to be leading an enterprise. The stress is real, but it comes from having too much to do and most likely from having too much business. The danger comes when the economy, your industry, and your company shift from Phase B, faster growth, to Phase C, a period of slower growth.

We cover Phases C and D in the next chapter. These phases encompass the backside, or downward slope, in the business cycle. A leader will need determination and steady nerves to make the most out of a deteriorating situation.

10 Playing Defense to Win

Enhancing Profits Even as the Economy Deteriorates

The previous chapter presented ITR's Management Objectives suited to economic and business expansion, Phases A and B of the business cycle. Each was geared to maximize profits and enhance the long-term position of the enterprise. This chapter presents Management Objectives that are defensive in nature but clearly designed to protect and enhance profits on the backside, or downward slope, in the business cycle—Phases C and D. We believe too many business leaders just learn new ways to say no on the downward slope (no to cash outlays, changes, and positive actions) as a hunker-down-and-wait attitude takes over in many corporate offices. We think positive, proactive action is required. Following are some thoughts that will help you in each decline between now and 2030 and in the depression to come.

Phase C occurs when the 12/12 rate-of-change has passed through a cyclical high and is descending toward the zero line. At this point, your quantity of business—measured in either volume or dollars—is still higher than it was the previous year, but increases are progressively declining. The 12/12 is on the backside of the business cycle and in the early portion of Phase C; the data trend's rate of ascent is slowing

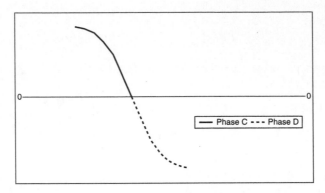

Figure 10.1   Phase C: 12/12 Is Declining toward Zero

Source: ITR Economics.

and will eventually move into steeper decline before Phase C is over, as shown in Figure 10.1.

Early Phase C is a great time in the business cycle because your cash flow is strong and your optimism remains high. You are the captain of a ship that's sailing smoothly at top speed. Everyone is delighted with how well things are going, including your customers, who are acting like they are still in Phase B.

Although it will take a while for the storm clouds to form in the distance, the leading indicators and rate-of-change tools have detected changes and warn you of the dangers that lie ahead. There are several typical reactions you want to avoid during this time, including:

- *The tendency to disregard the early signs* of impending economic problems as temporary matters that you can quickly and effectively control. Usually, outside authorities, such as the Federal Reserve, central banks, and governments, dismiss these first signals of change—much to their detriment.

- *The development of capacity constraints.* Management may be looking to quickly bring new, expensive capacity on line under the mistaken belief that the good times will continue indefinitely and customer demand will continue to grow. They won't.

- The *desire to expand core operations* and no longer be involved in acyclic or countercyclical markets. Because your company is making money and can barely meet the current demand, some of your people may not want to put resources into unproven areas.

Management Objectives

The overall theme here is *caution*. Be vigilant and prepare your company for less business in your current core businesses, lower profits, and erosion of your cash position. Make the best of Phase C by implementing the following steps. Read our shortened list of Management Objectives, select the ones that will work best for your business—and then *implement them*.

Cash Is Going to Be King

1. *Concentrate on the cash and balance sheet.* The best way to proceed is to remember the old but true maxim: *cash is king*. Because the bottom line is the most frequent and obvious measure of a chief executive officer's success, concentrate on it. However, prepare for slower growth and potential decline by giving your balance sheet a good hard look. Ask yourself the following questions as you do:
   a. Does your balance sheet depict a healthy company? If you check it and find room for improvement during the healthiest part of the business cycle, some heavy lifting might be required for the decline that lies ahead. You might have to pay off debt, beef up your cash position, and trim inventories.
   b. Do you have a depth of strength that you can draw upon in the coming quarters?
   c. Can you survive the next year if your business continues to soften and eventually starts to fall away? At what rate are you

burning through cash, and can you support spending at this rate in the future?

d. Will you be out of covenant on loan agreements? Make sure you can meet the terms of your loan agreements; you don't want to have liquidity problems because your lines of credit were withdrawn or called in during the next two years.

e. Will your debt-to-equity ratio prohibit you from borrowing more money in the potentially leaner months ahead? Because you want your business to expand, see if using leverage could be the best way to go. Expand at the bottom of the business cycle, when prices, including interest rates, are relatively low. Even though your business goes through Phase C or Phase D, you should be able to expand if you're not cash poor.

f. Are your receivables and payables under control? Are they current—and can you keep them that way? When cyclical conditions begin to deteriorate, many companies don't focus on keeping their receivables current. However, this must be ongoing in your company. Failure to manage your receivables can seriously harm your company as it heads into other phases of the business cycle.

Prepare for stormy waters as you answer these questions. Work with your accountant and finance team to come up with the best solutions. Who wants a leaky boat during a storm?

2. *Begin workforce reductions.* Many firms are "slow to fire and quick to hire." But Phase C's motto should be "quick to fire and slow to hire."

In Phase C, let them go.

In Phase A, bring them back.

Let natural attrition help you reduce your staff in early Phase C. Then complete the steps that follow to accomplish your goals of conserving cash and preparing for lower activity levels. Although it can be hard to let employees go, it's often necessary for your company's greater good. Ultimately, it may also be better for good employees who are on the wrong bus.

As your company progresses further into Phase C and conditions continue to soften, take the following steps:

a. Identify your A-, B-, and C-caliber personnel early in Phase C.

b. Set metrics to use to determine when the time comes to let people go, for example, when your 12/12 rate of change sinks to a 1 percent growth rate, when earnings before interest depreciation and amortization reach 3 percent, or when you foresee that you will have significant cash issues in another four months if you remain on your present course.

c. Make a list of the employees you will let go. Once you make this decision, much of the emotional pressures will subside, and you will have time to mentally prepare for the actual firing, which is always a difficult task. As businesses grow, it's normal for them to accumulate excess or less-than-stellar personnel, and trimming that fat is a normal and necessary management function.

3. *Set budget reduction goals by department.* Coming up with realistic budgets based on slower growth and the possibility of eventual decline may seem simple, but it can be difficult. For the past few years, your company's mantra may have been "growth, always growth," following the philosophy to "grow or die." However, the economic downturn will cause that growth to level off and contract. You must keep your expectations and resource allocations elastic enough to account for the changes that lie ahead.

Remember: *Home Depot doesn't stock snow shovels in the summer because they're not in demand.* Adjust your resources to cover not just a short seasonal period but also a cyclical period that could encompass a multitude of quarters—and keep in mind:

a. The anticipated cyclical demand should drive production schedules for people and machinery, raw material orders, and inventory levels for finished goods.

b. Changing business cycle conditions will also affect projected cash flow for both inbound and outbound needs. This means your ability to satisfy your creditors will be at stake. It could also affect your ability to make payroll.

c. Projected profitability and your ability to meet targets will determine how Wall Street, your board of directors, your business partners, or your other stakeholders react. In effect, they, or some combination of them, will judge your management capabilities regarding how well you utilize the factors of production and deliver profits in good or bad times.

d. Credibility with your customers, clients, staff, and suppliers will depend on how well you reach the goals you set. Make sure that you have metrics in place to determine when you achieve objectives and who within your organization is accountable for meeting them.

4. *Cut training.* Selectively put parts of your personnel training on hold. Although it makes no sense to train employees who may be working for someone else in a few months, your senior accounting staff may need continual training to stay current with new and ever-changing tax laws, regulations, and interpretations.

   If you find that lack of employee preparedness and capability is putting you at a competitive disadvantage, you may have to step up some training. Consider *cross-training* key people so that they can wear multiple hats and perform various tasks. For example, after taking a class or two, a less expensive junior executive might be able to handle more responsibility, or one of your warehouse workers could learn how to operate a forklift or your inventory control system.

Get All the Team on the Same Page

5. *Weed out inferior products.* Lose the losers. This process requires you to take a closer look and implement more draconian measures

than merely reducing or cutting back. Such products can be much like your beloved old Chevy, the one on which you and your siblings learned to drive, that still runs—barely. But it smokes like a chimney, eats up gas and oil, and isn't safe. You only dare to take it for very short rides. Although everyone has an emotional connection to it and doesn't want it to go, it takes up space, is rusting away, and serves no useful purpose. Get rid of it.

6. *Avoid long-term purchase commitments late in Phase C.* Prices for commodities and many other goods tend to move in conjunction with, or lag slightly behind, the four phases of the business cycle. Prices usually drop when the general economy is in Phase C and especially when it is moving into actual recession.

7. *Identify and overcome competitive disadvantages.* We dealt with the creation of competitive advantages in our discussions of Phase A and Phase B. Phase C is the time to identify and fix any competitive *disadvantage* as you head further down the business cycle slope. Competitive disadvantages can cause you to lose customers for reasons, such as:

   a. Slow deliveries.

   b. Poor or barely adequate quality.

   c. Dated brands and messages. For example, don't encourage your customers to put a tiger in their tank. Instead, tell them to move into the increased mileage world.

   d. Not using the latest and expected technology. As a survey company, are you using a laser transit with a handheld computer-recording device? Is your data processing as efficient or as up to date as your competitors'? Are you the last gas station not accepting debit cards?

   e. Packaging that customers view as environmentally unfriendly or wasteful.

8. *Make sure you and the management teams are not in denial.* If straight-line forecasting becomes a group event—which can

easily happen—it can lead to all kinds of budgetary and resource allocation problems. Like most problems, the cure for these matters is best when you apply them in a preventative fashion. Keep your team aware of the internal and external rates of change, leading indicators, and industry forecasts to build credibility and teamwork—and keep everyone in the loop.

9. *Watch accounts receivables*. Pay close attention to aging receivables. Don't let your past due ratio grow faster than your sales. Phase C is an ideal time to listen to your accounting staff when they tell you to be careful with how much credit you extend and to whom you extend it.

   Be prepared to deal with the competing interests of the good folks in the sales and accounting departments:

   a. Sales has a pedal-to-the-metal mind-set and wants to bring in orders through any means, including extending the most favorable credit terms.

   b. Accounting can see that many of today's sales will be tomorrow's collection problems when the economy deteriorates and eventually moves into Phase D.

   You can't make everybody happy. However, remember this:

   a. If you *lose a sale* because the potential customer didn't have good enough credit, it will cost you only the *profit you would have made on that sale*.

   b. If you make the sale and subsequently have to write off the entire sale amount as uncollectible, it will cost you more. The amount you lose could be equal to the profit from many sales.

10. *Increase the requirements to justify capital expenditures*. It's tempting to spend money on more in late Phase B and early Phase C—because everything is going well and everyone is optimistic then. Denial may even take hold when caution signs appear because everyone is positive that they can keep the good times going forever if they just:

a. Add more people

b. Buy more equipment

c. Upgrade systems

Many companies will add all sorts of items in early Phase C— a plant, another shift, a new line of automated equipment, a new fleet of trucks, or a new computer system—all because of the mistaken belief that this will keep the good times rolling. These expenditures can sow the seeds for future cash crunches that can force you into bankruptcy or unwanted mergers.

Instead, invest your capital to *push into new markets*—and spend on items that will give you a quick payback and have the potential to bring in more cash, such as extensions to your existing capabilities, green offshoots of your business, new, more efficient equipment, export markets, and aftermarket service.

11. *Evaluate vendors for strength.* Make sure that your vendors are financially and operationally solid. Find out if they can survive Phase C and Phase D by asking the following about each supplier:

a. Does the management team understand what is going on in the economy and in the industry?

b. Is it adding fixed costs and shelling out cash based on the mistaken assumption that the good times will last through the next two years?

Keep an eye on your distributors. Their health is important to you, and it's essential that they can supply what you need on time. Encourage them to think about cutting their inventories. If your vendors are financially weak and in danger of failing, it could leave you with the expensive problem of covering the services and warranties that they would normally provide. When your suppliers can't deliver to you, you may not be able to deliver to your customers or clients. And if your vendors go under, it could quickly put you at a serious competitive disadvantage and drain your cash.

Phase D—The Most Negative Phase of the Cycle

Phase D of the business cycle is when your 12/12 rate-of-change is declining below the zero line and your 12 monthly moving total (12MMT) of revenue (or whatever other data series you track) is moving lower (see Figure 10.2). Emotions run high during Phase D. People have different feelings on different days and their responses will vary:

- "This is only a temporary, short-term deviation."
- "The economy is not a factor; *we* can stop this slide any time."
- "Nothing has changed. We're not going through difficult times." (These three people are in denial.)
- "It's the big one and we're done for now." The fair-weather, inexperienced managers have been listening to way too much news. Some of them are paralyzed, and the others head for the lifeboats.
- "Okay, yes, the seas will be getting rough, so let's ready the ship, adjust our course, and keep moving." These are our heroes—the ones who stay calm, acknowledge reality, and adjust without losing their way or giving up on their dreams.

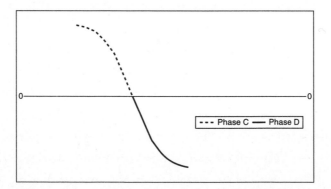

Figure 10.2 Phase D: 12/12 Descending Further and Further below Zero

Source: ITR Economics.

Phase D Management Objectives

You can ready the ship, keep it sailing on course, and navigate out of danger by following our Management Objectives explained next.

Despite declining revenues, companies can remain profitable in Phase D—and position themselves for the future by carrying out the following Management Objectives:

Less is More

- *Reduce advertising; be very selective.* We understand the value of keeping your company's name in front of the buying public. However, we question the wisdom of expending money on advertising during difficult times in light of the limited return on investment that it produces. For example, why should a home-building company, such as D. R. Horton, spend $15 million on advertising when its brand is strong and the housing market has virtually dried up? What purpose would its advertising serve?

   On the other hand, it makes sense for an automobile dealership to advertise its superior service department and offer specials that will bring in more revenue by bringing people into its showroom while their tires are being rotated. If advertising will drive revenues, it can be a wise move.

- *Avoid long-term purchasing commitments.* If you're used to locking in costs with long-term contracts, you must account for the fact that the prices for most goods and many services tend to follow the business cycle downward. So limit your inventory purchases when the economy is in Phase D. Buying less will allow you to keep a handle on your costs and give yourself some wiggle room on your selling price. If you can give your customers price breaks, they will appreciate that benefit—and it won't negatively affect *your* bottom line.

- *Review all lease agreements.* Vacancies go up during recession or Phase D; therefore, property owners can have problems with their cash flow if their debt services, taxes, insurance, and maintenance costs are not elastic. These property owners want stable paying tenants—thereby allowing you to strike good deals and create win-win situations.

- *Increase your requirements for capital expenditures.* In the first half of Phase D, only a few good reasons exist to buy capital equipment:
  a. The equipment will push your company into new markets that will offset the decline in your core activity.
  b. The equipment has a long lead time; that is, you have to order it now for it to be ready for Phase A.
  c. The current cash savings are too good to pass up. You can obtain savings from getting better terms, increased efficiencies, and new processes or decreased labor, to name just a few.
  d. The equipment will provide you with a great technological advantage that will help drive prospects to you.

  Near the bottom of Phase D, look at acquiring new and used capital equipment that can help you succeed in Phase A. The cost of capital equipment late in Phase D will be less than it was in early Phase D. By waiting until that time, the profits you will make in the years to come will reward your patience many times over.

- *Combine departments with like capabilities and reduce management.* Look at your entire organization with an eye toward streamlining its operations and organizational structure. You may have added capabilities and made room for specialties and compartmentalized operations in Phase B, which turned out to be smart moves. However, now that you're in Phase D, you may need to deconstruct what you carefully put together in Phase B.

  For instance, you may have made some changes if you operate an insurance agency that grew briskly from 2002 to 2008 along with the economy. As the economy roared, you added staff to serve construction companies, to sell to the medical industry, and to develop and sell financial planning products for young couples just starting out in life. You gave each group a support staff, a sales staff, and a group supervisor, all of which were necessary in the flurry of Phase B. Now that Phase D has arrived, you need to examine whether three separate support staffs and three supervisors still make sense—especially because the people who serve the construction industry are desperately trying to look busy whenever you walk by. Now is the time to combine groups and protect your bottom line.

- *Tighten credit policies; increase scrutiny.* Take two important steps that your salespeople probably won't appreciate. First, reformulate your credit policies to fit the times. Raise credit score requirements and those for balance sheet ratios before extending credit to new or existing (but marginally profitable) customers. Second, watch your receivables and don't be shy about trying to collect on time and cutting off credit when customers fall behind. Your accounting department will back this up: you can't afford to be lax when extending credit.

Time to Open Up the Purse Strings

- *Grab distressed competitors' market share.* Firms that were caught off guard by the recession will have the greatest difficulty keeping pace. As Phase D drags on, they will find the following areas especially difficult:
  a. Innovation
  b. Introduction of new products
  c. Development and declaration of competitive advantages
  d. Marketing
  e. Advertising and promotions aimed at those that are still buying

  Struggling firms will know there are willing and able customers in the marketplace, but they will lack the advertising and promotion budgets to attract their attention and make the sale.

Competitors with cash will have the firepower to take away market share from firms that are caught off guard.

- *Think about buying commercial property.* By the time you're in late Phase D, you will have a good handle on when the macroeconomic recovery will begin. As it now stands, commercial property construction and property prices are still lagging behind U.S. industrial production. In addition, interest rates are always lowest during late Phase D of the business cycle—and most people won't recognize that a recovery has begun until we are at least one quarter into the recovery. Late Phase D provides a great opportunity, because commercial property prices will be lower than they have been in years, interest rates will be favorable, and the economy will be improving.

- *Be open to the probabilities of a developing recovery.* Through analysis of your own rates of change, have the foresight to see that the initial signs of improving business for the company are consistent with what the leading indicators have been telling you should be happening. When these two factors are in sync, don't be afraid to start spending some money in anticipation of the upturn.

- *Seize on opportunistic purchases of other companies.* The doom and gloom of the last few quarters still prevail. Interest rates remain low and people's expectations are even lower. Many firms have run out of cash or will very soon. Others are depressed, are discouraged, and are losing their will to fight as the recession drags on. As a result, many will be increasingly willing to sell their businesses or parts of them.

  Now is the time to act. Start looking for firms in distress, and begin conversations to purchase them or parts of them. Look to buy companies that would be good fits with your current operation and provide the most positive impact on your business in the next few years.

The Rules Are Changing

Demographic, financial, and technology shifts—along with cultural changes—provide a lot of the fodder for the changing economics we discuss in this book. A library of books has been written on the inevitability of change, how to contend with it, and how to manage it. Our goal in writing this book has been to make it increasingly probable that you will profit through the coming changes. One of the most difficult series of changes to manage is the business cycle, because the extant reasons why a cycle will occur change from one cycle to the next. That is why this chapter and the previous one briefly discussed how to establish a process for measuring business cycle change as a routine part of managing the business. Integrating business cycle management with your strategic visions as we head toward 2030 will ensure that you are maximizing your profits in business and in your portfolio.

Following are our top 10 rules for profiting through one business cycle to the next.

Top 10 Rules for Managing the Business Cycle

1. Realize that your business and that of your customers and clients are subject to the influences of cyclical change.

2. Develop objective means of measuring changes in your company's rate of growth.

3. Always know what phase of the business cycle your company is in and whether it is in the beginning, middle, or end of that phase.

4. Understand where each of your markets is in the business cycle and whether it is leading or lagging.

5. Develop and learn how to use a system of leading indicators to project your company's future.

6. Develop a culture within your company that understands that change is a continual process and that is dedicated to keeping your company evolving with your markets.

7. Ask yourself on a regular basis, "What *don't* I know?"

8. Find markets that are relatively acyclic or affected to a less-than-average degree by business cycles.

9. Understand that your personnel will tend to resist change and that you must be prepared to lead with certainty and clarity.

10. Be willing to adapt your business practices and procedures quickly in accordance with changes in the business cycle and your markets.

Summary

Attitudes can become quite negative on the back side of the business cycle. Sluggish economic environments, recessions, and a depression will do that to people. The best leaders will stay realistic but also optimistic, exude that optimism, and implement strategies that enhance the company's position now and for years to come. It will take a large dose of self-confidence, a lot of communication, and a firm handle on where you are in the business cycle.

11 Great Opportunities within the Stock Market

What Businesses and Individuals Need to Know

It would be great to be able to list five must-have stocks for the period between now and 2030. But life doesn't work that way because circumstances change, interests vary, and capabilities fluctuate—stock prices even moreso in the short term. Instead, we are going to lay out what we think are going to be exciting business and personal investment *sectors* for you to consider in the coming years. The point of listing these areas is not to see whether you are already doing business in any of them but for you to ask yourself, "How *can* I do business in that market going forward?" This is consistent with one of our favorite quotes from the late W. Edwards Deming, eminent scholar and teacher in American academia: "It is not necessary to change. Survival is not mandatory." It is also consistent with the question we are very fond of asking: What's next? To change is not only to survive but also to give yourself a chance to grow and succeed even more rapidly than you have in the past. See if you can't discover or, even better, invent a way to participate in one of the following trends.

As individuals, we can participate in the growth of some of these opportunistic sectors by making them a part of our investment portfolios. Whether they form a core part of your portfolio or are satellite investments is entirely up to you. What follows is a listing of exchange traded funds (ETFs) that relate to several of the opportunistic sectors described. The ETFs' inclusion here is not an offer to buy or to sell, nor are these recommendations. They are merely examples of ETFs you may want to consider if any of these sectors intrigues you. The ETFs listed later in this chapter are provided as examples courtesy of our friend and money manager Clark Bellin of Lincoln, Nebraska (cbellin@mundy andassociates.com).

Energy Distribution

Energy distribution is a classic way to benefit from growth while hedging price risk. Until the transportation devices of *Star Trek* fame become a reality, there will always be a need to get a product from point A to point B. Doing so efficiently is profitable work. We focus on energy distribution because the world's energy needs will continue to grow in relation to economic growth. There is a lot of money to make by investing in wellheads and power plants; however, we like the less price-sensitive and less variable income that streams from bringing the energy from the proverbial source to the consumer.

This is what makes TransCanada a longtime favorite stock holding. In today's environment of wide-open energy development across the globe—something hydraulic fracturing in the United States especially exemplifies—the need to get the product from the ground to the consumer is *fundamental*. In North Dakota, like many other places, people are burning off the excess natural gas that is a byproduct of wells. By law or because of economics, that gas is going to be harvested and piped to consumers elsewhere. In 2013, the United States passed Russia in terms of daily production of barrels of crude oil. This is the beginning. The need to get the crude to refineries, get the crude from refineries to power plants, and get the electricity from power plants to consumers is a compelling economic picture. Determine whether there isn't a way for you to be part of that picture.

Look at PowerShares Dynamic Oil and Gas Services Portfolio (trading symbol PXJ), an energy services ETF. Whether it suits your needs or not, it is a place to start. In February 2014, the diversification available to any individual interested in this economic sector is evidenced by the major holdings of this ETF:

Baker Hughes Inc.

Schlumberger Ltd.

Halliburton Co.

National Oilwell Varco Inc.

Oceaneering International Inc.

Weatherford International Ltd.

Transocean Ltd.

Noble Corp. PLC

Patterson-UTI Energy Inc.

Tesco Corp.

Printed Electronics

Low cost, flexible, smart, useful, cool, and growing—the production of printed electronics uses standard or slightly modified printing equipment, utilized on substrates ranging from film to fabric. The ink is semiconducting organic-based material. Think flexible rolls of transistors and resistors for appliance displays, clothing that lights up and changes color or pattern based on your mood or physical needs, smart(er) watches and other jewelry, newspapers and magazines whose headlines are animated and constantly updated, building windows that vary the amount of light and heat that come through, better batteries, flexible lighting elements, e-wallpaper, e-paper, advanced games, packaging options, smart tags, smart labeling, and quarterbacks who wouldn't need eight inches of plays wrapped around their nonthrowing forearm!

Market size estimates vary because the field is relatively broad from a definitional standpoint and expanding so fast. ThomasNet News reports that IDTechEx (an industry source) estimated that the market for printed, organic, and flexible electronics will grow from just under $17 billion today to more than $76 billion by 2023. Such dollar growth will put it on par with the size of the global machine tool industry of today.

Not only do today's printing companies and print machinery providers need to focus on this market; just think about the new materials, applications, and delivery systems wrapped around this concept. Use your imagination and be part of the future.

Mexico

We like Mexico's economic prospects going forward. As the world's fourteenth-largest economy in 2012, it is only going to get bigger, fast. This southern neighbor will benefit the U.S. economy's growth, its own favorable demographic trend, an impressive natural resource base to see it through the minefield of inflation, and an apparent newfound openness to outside investment in exploiting those natural resources. In addition, Mexico is a natural geographic link between north and south in the Americas. Although violence via gangs and drug cartels tends to dominate the headlines about Mexico, we can look beyond that to see a burgeoning manufacturing base that is going to diversify the economy and has the potential to create a middle class in a country too long characterized by income extremes. From a business perspective, we are hard-pressed to see how you can ignore exploring the possibilities of doing business in Mexico other than just as a tourist.

Doing business in Mexico is not for every firm, but we can all entertain the notion of benefiting from the country's encouraging economic prospects. An ETF to look at here is iShares MSCI Mexico Capped ETF (trading symbol EWW). The major holdings within this ETF as of February 2014 include:

America Movil SAB de CV

Fomento Económico Mexicano SAB

Grupo Financiero Banorte SAB de CV

Grupo Televisa SAB

Cemex SAB de CV

Grupo Mexico SAB de CV

Alfa SAB de CV

Wal-Mart de Mexico SAB de CV

Grupo Financiero Inbursa SAB

Fibra Uno Administracion SA

Water Conservation and Distribution

Despite seemingly endless warnings to the contrary, we aren't going to run out of water. Israel has found a way to make do with relatively little, as have other parts of the world—and the United States and other economies will find themselves learning from the Israelis of the world in terms of water management. It is like crude oil; despite peak oil proclamations, the world is not going to run out of oil. We will simply start pricing and conserving such resources to ensure we don't run out. And in fact, it is in the pricing, conserving, and seeking new sources that the economic opportunities lie for the future. Whether it is improved desalinization, piping water from the Great Lakes region of the United States, floating icebergs, and so on, processes abound for ensuring this supply of our most precious natural resource. We suspect that the solution to the supply issue will vary from one geographic site to the next across the planet, unless a new, cheap energy source for desalinization is discovered in the near term.

This sector is an emotional hot button for a lot of people, from environmentalists to social planners to the farmers who bring us our food. We personally have no interest in piping and trucking water from one part of the country to another. That doesn't mean we cannot be a player in this arena via our portfolio using the PowerShares Water Resources Portfolio ETF, whose trading symbol is PHO and whose major holdings in February 2014 were:

> Waters Corp.
>
> Pentair Ltd.
>
> Xylem Inc./NY
>
> Flowserve Corp.
>
> Roper Industries Inc.
>
> Lindsay Corp.
>
> Valmont Industries Inc.
>
> American Water Works Co. Inc.
>
> Aqua America Inc.
>
> Mueller Water Products Inc.

Health Care

It is projected that there will be a billion more people on our planet before 2050. Some two-thirds of all the people who were ever 65 years or older are alive today. These numbers tell us that whether one focuses on the very young, the aging population, or anywhere in between, there is an expanding need for health care in the future. Layer on top of that the expanding middle class worldwide and the accordant improvement in the standard of living, and you have a viable marketplace for the future.

Because of the U.S. government's increasing involvement in the health care system, we aren't sure that being United States–centric in this field will be especially lucrative—unless it is in the private health care delivery tier of the marketplace. But putting aside how profitable the field is going to be, it *is* going to be a stable and organically growing product and services industry worldwide. Keep in mind that other countries are rapidly developing their medical care capabilities as well as seeing population growth. Look beyond North America and Europe for your opportunities and into Asia, Central America, and South America for exciting quests toward growth.

Manufacturing medical devices, generating body parts, providing lab services, training health practitioners, and being involved with fundamental research is but a small sampling of the ways we can be involved in this segment of economic activity on an enterprise level. But perhaps the iShares U.S. Healthcare ETF (trading symbol IYH) intrigues you. Its major holdings in February 2014 were:

Johnson & Johnson

Pfizer Inc.

Merck & Co. Inc.

Gilead Sciences Inc.

Amgen Inc.

Bristol-Myers Squibb Co.

AbbVie Inc.

Biogen Idec Inc.

UnitedHealth Group Inc.

Celgene Corp.

Vocational Education

This sector is a bit more of a niche than the preceding ones. Our thinking here is that there is a yawning gap between the type of work skills we need in many economies, the type of education we provide in the United States, and the social pressure to want to see our kids do better than we did and, hence, have more clean hands and white collar jobs. What the industrialized world—particularly in the West—is in short supply of are artisans who know how to work with their heads and their hands. We need computer numerical control operators, welders, truck drivers, manufacturers, technicians, and so on, today—and we'll need them in the future. These are noble occupations that we have not been training enough people to perform, at a time when four-year colleges and universities are pricing themselves beyond so many people's reach. There seems to be a skill-training gap, particularly in the United States, that will be filled by vocational training and by one- and two-year highly specialized certificate programs coupled with better internship and apprentice programs to get people the experience they need to be truly marketable.

3-D Printing

3-D printing is sometimes called additive manufacturing. It allows for both prototype and low-volume local production of parts ranging in material structure from polymers to metals. This industry has the potential to revolutionize inventory control, distribution of finished parts, and raw materials. The production of intricate and durable products is a reality today, and the ability to make increasingly complex assemblies of various parts is on the horizon. The industry was estimated to be about $2 billion (in 2012), including equipment, software, and services—and most folks in this arena expect it to grow by about 150 percent between now and 2018–2020.

The equipment that makes the 3-D printed output a reality is inexpensive to acquire. The software is out there but is not ubiquitous.

We wouldn't be surprised if you someday go on Amazon.com to acquire and download a piece of software that will enable you to replicate or replace the broken door handle on your car, light cover, or button or switch on your electronic equipment, or buy custom-made souvenirs, employee and customer appreciation awards, airplane parts—the list goes on and on. Figure out now how your customers or some potential customers could benefit from you employing this technology.

Housing

Soon, there will be 1 billion more people on this planet—100 million of those in the United States alone, and they'll all require shelter. You can choose to be a part of the supply chain that eventually becomes shelter for an individual or a family. Sometimes it isn't any more complicated than that.

Security

The world is becoming an increasingly accessible place, physically and electronically. With this accessibility come physical and electronic perils that are a natural result of the less-than-saintly side of human nature. Including guards, alarm companies, armed protection, investigation, special hardware, cyber protection, and armored vehicles, this is a huge global industry—estimated to be about $170 billion globally in recent years. And it's growing at a pace that we think will outstrip global gross domestic product growth by several percentage points each year.

Although the margins in some aspects of this industry likely aren't great, it is a bit like the hedge fund industry, where you count on dollar volume while sucking up nickels. It is a big world out there—and there are a lot of nickels to garner. The preceding really is a personal or corporate security focus. The issue of national security and the money governments spend makes the previous slice of the industry look like the minor leagues. A problem with the national security side of the industry is the inconsistency of government funding for what seems like wide swathes of the products and services proffered for sale. Today's hero who is providing armor plating for a vehicle the infantry uses could be on the outs just as easily as an aircraft manufacturer or the company making the connectors for the electronics on ships. The private sector may have to contend with the vagaries of the business cycle, but the national security side has to consider the business cycle *and* the whims of government. You may prefer this because of margins, order sizes, or patriotic fervor, but it certainly is a different means of making a living.

Natural Resources

Inflation is destined to be part of our economic future. Along with global economic and population growth, inflation is going to make the harvesting and conservation of natural resources a winning arena. You'll want to focus on countries that own the natural resources and companies that are very good at responsibly bringing them to market. Think beyond food and trees and instead about ores, petroleum products, and the building blocks of nanostructures. The iShares North American Natural Resources ETF (trading symbol IGE) cited later is too heavily weighted toward energy resources to be ideal in our view, but it gives you a starting point. Perhaps you would want to round this holding out with an ETF that focuses on agricultural commodities, renewable energy, or industrial metals. IGE's major holdings in February 2014 were:

Exxon Mobil Corp.

Chevron Corp.

Schlumberger Ltd.

ConocoPhillips

Occidental Petroleum Corp.

Suncor Energy Inc.

EOG Resources Inc.

Halliburton Co.

Phillips 66

Anadarko Petroleum Corp.

Food

The demographics are there: more food, please. Growing it is near the beginning of the issue; getting it where it is necessary is another factor. Variations in climate across the globe will make the food industry anything but boring going forward. Boundless opportunities exist in this arena, whether it is because you are involved with genetically modified (or genetically pure) foodstuffs, catering to health conscious trends, making a fortune trading pork bellies, or selling modern irrigation equipment as fresh water becomes higher priced.

PowerShares Dynamic Food and Beverage Portfolio ETF's (trading symbol PBJ) February 2014 holdings offer some clues regarding where we might conceivably make some money in the future as businesses and as individuals. You just have to love a food-related ETF whose trading symbol is PBJ.

The Hershey Co.

Archer Daniels Midland Co.

Mondelez International Inc.

General Mills Inc.

Green Mountain Coffee Roasters

PepsiCo Inc.

The Coca-Cola Co.

Starbucks Corp.

The Kroger Co.

Tyson Foods Inc.

Entertainment

It has been said that Western civilization will never notice its ultimate demise because we will have been so busy entertaining ourselves. If a hallmark of a growing middle class is increasing leisure time, then finding a means to be part of the entertainment industry seems desirable. Entertainment in our context is more than just the traditional leisure industry. It would have to include motor sports, athletic endeavors, bowling, electronic games, and so on—whatever people like to do to consume their free time that requires an outlay of cash. We want to be there. As economists, the concept of entertainment is somewhat foreign to us, so we contemplate the PowerShares Dynamic Leisure and Entertainment Portfolio ETF's (trading symbol PEJ) major holdings as of February 2014 (Note that Papa John's and Starbucks make the list. Eating is also entertainment!):

Wynn Resorts Ltd.

The Walt Disney Co.

Las Vegas Sands Corp.

Starwood Hotels & Resorts World

Scripps Networks Interactive Inc.

Priceline.com Inc.

Time Warner Inc.

Starbucks Corp.

Royal Caribbean Cruises Ltd.

Papa John's International Inc.

12 Investing Based on Age and Trend

Some Commonalities

Both of this book's authors are registered investment advisors. What that means to you is that we know enough to be dangerous and are savvy enough to know what we don't know. Therefore, this chapter won't be about how to make your millions through investing or giving you tips on beating the market. Rather, it will teach you how to use the trends that we see coming over the next 25 years to your advantage. We don't believe in get-rich-quick schemes (unless of course, you are just plain lucky). I (Brian) once read a very interesting math book that postulated that there *must* indeed be a phenomenon known as beginner's luck. The book maintained that it had to exist—because why else would so many people think they can consistently beat the odds in activities such as the stock market, horse racing, cards, roulette, and the like? Many of these people must have had relatively successful initial forays into these endeavors for them to keep trying. So if you are one of these truly lucky people, feel free to skip this chapter. But read on if you want to try to improve your odds of making money by using economic trends and proven approaches.

We placed this chapter at this specific point in the book because understanding the driving economic forces that lie ahead is crucial to making money in the *long term*. This differs from investing for overnight wins (for people who are lucky or smarter than we are) or investing for success over the course of a single business cycle (strategies change on the rise and the decline and to a certain extent from one business cycle to the next). This is investing for the long haul, by which we mean at least two business cycles (a minimum of six years) and no longer than five business cycles (a maximum of 20 years). To do this successfully requires a disciplined investor—that is, someone who isn't easily swayed from a particular course because of short-term adversity or surprisingly positive returns. You are not disciplined if you suffer losses for a year and give up on an approach. (However, you *are* likely a latent market timer.) You also aren't disciplined if you make outsized gains in one area one year and thus decide to shift more of your money into that area. There are other aspects that comprise the discipline of investing that we'll touch on a little later in the context of age categories.

We have learned through the years that asset allocation is essential to investing successfully. This differs from simply diversifying your portfolio; *diversification* means having investments in equities spread among multiple industries, for instance stock positions in banks, consumer durables, and energy. Remember to keep the diversification tied to the general themes of demographics, inflation, and taxes. *Asset allocation* means having some money in equities, some money in fixed income, some in real estate, and some in other alternative investments, such as precious metals, art, stock options, and so on. Keep this basic concept in mind as you build an investment around this core of proper asset allocation. It will allow you to develop satellite investments that represent your hunches, bets, mad money, or I-am-going-to-beat-the-market money. If you are wise, you start with a solid core—maybe as much as 80 percent to 100 percent of your portfolio—and gradually expand into the satellite arena once you are on a path to financial solvency.

The core is what you will eventually depend upon for your retirement income, so it really should be the vast majority of your portfolio.

But if, like a lot of entrepreneurs, you are young or otherwise impatient, you will tend to have your core investments but also a much larger minority of your money in these satellites. Within each of these buckets—which include equities, fixed income, real estate, and so on—you will want to diversify to mitigate short-term risk and maximize long-term return. A truly excellent book on this topic called *7Twelve: A Diversified Investment Portfolio with a Plan* was written by a friend of mine (Brian) named Craig Israelsen. Craig is a PhD and Executive-in-Residence in the Financial Planning Program at Utah Valley University, Orem, Utah. Prior to teaching at UVU he taught at BYU and University of Missouri–Columbia. If you like the wisdom and comfort of mathematics and logic and want to make money, his book is a must read.

There are only four things—only four—that any of us can do with our money. That is it. We can:

1. Spend it.
2. Invest it.
3. Save it.
4. Give it away.

If you think we should add a fifth category—pay taxes—that comes under either spending or giving it away, depending on how you feel about what you get for your tax dollars.

Doing all four is normal and healthy; what the right proportions are is a personal choice. The tendency when we are young is to spend a greater portion of our income and save and invest less. This is because we normally want or need things. Although it's understandable and likely something more people do, it is nonetheless a mistake (more on this later).

There is a huge difference between *spending* and *investing*. Spending requires you to put out some cash, receive an asset or experience in return, and eventually end up with less cash than you initially put out. An investment involves an initial outlay of cash, too, but the intent is to eventually end up with *more* cash than you initially put out. Buying a car is a classic example of an instance in which spending and investing are intentionally blurred. You spend money to buy a car and will constantly be spending money to *maintain* that car. In return, you get transportation—which may enable you to make an income or it may not. One thing is for sure: unless you are an automobile collector, you are not going to get the money that you put into the car (purchase price and maintenance) when you go to sell it. This is why it drives us crazy when a car salesperson tries to sell us some additional service under the premise of protecting an investment. If all of our investments worked out as well as this depreciating asset that requires a constant infusion of cash, we would be eating Alpo when we retire.

Spending is for *current consumption*, because we get some utility from that asset in the here and now. Investing requires that we forego the here and now to have more money in the future. Should you buy a Chevy instead of a Bentley because of this argument? *Absolutely*, if you don't have enough money building for the future—but absolutely *not* if you are already prepared for that future and wish to enjoy the finer things in life for yourself.

Note that we also distinguish between investing and saving. We are strong advocates that you should have sufficient liquid assets set aside (cash saved) to cover your expenses for three to six months in the event that you lose your income. Once you've established this nest egg, you then start putting significant dollars into a portfolio that is relatively illiquid. You don't want to have to sell your stocks, bonds, or other investments at an inopportune time because of a relatively short-term liquidity issue. Savings may be in the form of bank accounts, lumpy mattresses stuffed with cash, short-term Treasury bills, short-term certificates of deposit, or money market funds.

How much to give away is a deeply personal choice. Most tax systems encourage you to employ tax deductions for the amount you give away, but if that is your sole motivation for giving, you can probably find more efficient means of paying less in taxes. Most of us hand over our hard-earned dollars because it helps others and makes us feel good about ourselves in the process. Sometimes it is a self-acknowledgment of how fortunate we are. Of course, the exact amount you should or could give away is beyond the scope of this book.

Finally, many folks invest for their retirement using some sort of 401(k) or other tax-efficient means. Using these tax vehicles makes sense for most, but not every investor; it depends on your age and what you think will be happening in the future. We'll go into more detail on this later in this chapter.

Different Markets—Different Times

Asset allocation is critical because asset classes are frequently *uncorrelated*; that is, one may be doing well whereas others are doing poorly. Broad economic trends can also define this relative performance— which is something we are going to look at briefly before getting into some age-driven guidelines.

Keep in mind that we think asset allocation makes all the sense in the world. We are simply advocating overweighting and under-weighting *certain* asset classes based on the major economic trends we see ahead.

Figure 12.1 illustrates the post-WWII history of the S&P 500 Index, which is not adjusted for inflation on this graph. The S&P 500, also known as the Standard & Poor's 500, is compiled by S&P Dow Jones Indices. Note that the history is plotted on log scale so that the most recent experience isn't distorted by the sheer heights to which the S&P 500 has ascended. *Log scale* allows us to look at the percent change in value through time. The chart shows that there has been a

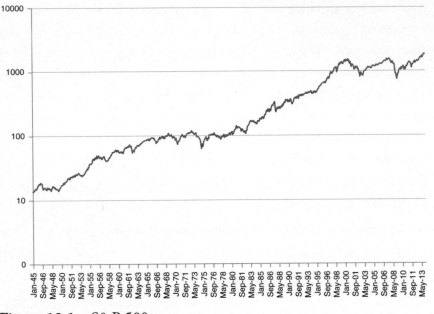

Figure 12.1   S&P 500

Source: S&P Dow Jones indices.

high degree of volatility in the market via the large swings down and up since 1998. We can see that, relatively speaking, the period from the August 2000 high to year-end 2013 was quiet, with the index gaining 21.8 percent over just a little longer than 12 years. Compare that with the prior 12 years, ending in August 2000—when the S&P 500 rose 480.3 percent. The period we have been living through for the past decade or so has been a more volatile version of the late 1960s and 1970s, when the S&P 500 last experienced a major flat period.

A question arises: Should we overweight stocks going forward because we are about to enter another exciting ascent like the 1950s, 1980s, and 1990s, or underweight stocks because we will get more of the lackluster same going forward as we have in the recent past? With massive liquidity having been injected into the world's economy since 2008, extremely low interest rates, and consumers generally in good financial shape, the odds seem to favor assuming that a better long-term trend lies ahead. However, our view is that you can't know the answer for certain—which is why you approach the equity market one way if you are within 10 years of retirement and view it from an appreciably different perspective when you are 40 years from retirement. As you grow closer to retirement age, you can't really risk having your capital decrease in nominal terms or be eroded by inflation's effects. At this point in your life, you need steady and reliable income. However, when you have four decades or more to grow your money, you take your shots and rest in the knowledge that the stock market is a great place to make money over the long run.

Most people should always be in the stock market. The questions are to what degree and how you invest, whether you're protecting the profits you've made, and what you are looking to get out of the investment. The answers to these issues depend on your age—something we'll discuss more later.

Equities (stocks) look like long-term winners. Bonds come under the heading of fixed-income investments. In this situation, you lend your money to some entity—a corporation, a government, or a person—and it pays you interest on the principal you lent to it, as well as the principal value in total when the bond matures. There are exceptions—such as zero-coupon bonds, which don't pay interest along the way. Instead they are initially sold at a deep discount with the face value of the bond paid at maturity. But most bonds pay interest along the way.

It has become dogma that it is wise as we age to move money *out of stocks* and *into bonds*. After all, the principal will be returned to you eventually, and you get a fixed amount of income in the form of interest payments while you wait. This bit of investment creed has worked out well for the last 30 years; however, it may not work out as well in the next 20 years or so. Unlike the last 30 years, when bond prices were generally rising, we are moving into a future that will more closely

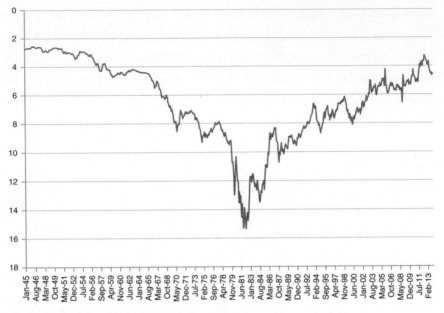

Figure 12.2   Monthly AAA-Rated Corporate Bond Prices

Source: Federal Reserve Board.

resemble the 1950s through the 1970s. Look at Figure 12.2 to see what a difference the reference to time makes.

One of the advantages to studying history is that although you learn that things change, you notice that they usually change into something similar to what we have seen in the past. We think the period from 2014 through 2030 will generally resemble the 1950–1970 trend—because *inflation*, not deflation, will be the defining characteristic. Deflation, or disinflation—meaning lower and lower interest rates resulting in higher and higher bond prices—dominated the world economy in the 1980s through 2013 (and perhaps a little beyond). Inflation means increasingly higher interest rates, resulting in increasingly lower bond prices.

The impact for us going forward is clear: if inflation is coming, buying bonds as an investment—and assuming that we can simply sell those bonds for a profit when we need the money in the future—is erroneous. You will have to hold your bonds until they mature during the coming inflation to ensure you get your principal back—and that assumes the issuing entity has not gone bankrupt. You can no longer take for granted that you will be able to sell your bond for a profit when you retire, when the kids go to college, or if a financial emergency arises. That leaves many bond mutual funds out in the cold, because they *don't* mature; they have a constantly turning over portfolio of bonds. But as was the case in the 1970s, you will be hard-pressed to see the portfolio's sum value of bonds go up when interest rates do. Bond fund net asset values are going to face a near-constant economic headwind called inflation as we head toward the next Great Depression because of the inflation driver—and its myriad sources that we have already discussed in this book.

Figure 12.3 presents the recent history of home prices in the United States. Given the demographic probabilities of the United States, Europe, and parts of Asia (including Russia), it's prudent to focus on

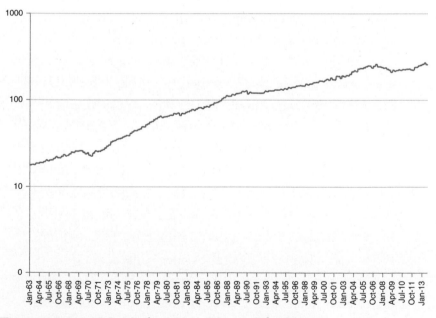

Figure 12.3   U.S. Median New Home Sales Price

Source: National Association of Realtors.

U.S. home prices going forward. The best price appreciation is going to occur where demand—that is, population—is growing. The history of rising home prices from 1963 to date is clear—with the exception of recessions in the early 1970s, early 1990s, and the Great Recession of 2008. General economic recessions will cause disruptions in the rising trend for home prices, and similar disruptions will take place in the future. What is *not* likely to recur between now and 2030 is the significant break in prices that occurred in conjunction with the Great Recession of 2008. So don't let temporary potholes in a prolonged rising trend dissuade you from making investments in this arena. Just be sure to focus on the three economic equivalents to location, location, and location: water, views, and urban.

Another friend of ours named Scott Stewart is a whiz at hedging and makes several very useful observations about what to do at the end of the rising trend in home prices. According to Scott:

> While an astute person might sell off a vacation home at the peak of an inflationary cycle, few people want to sell their main residence. An aggressive solution would be to short a real estate ETF [exchange traded fund] like iShares U.S. Real Estate (trading symbol IYR) or short stocks on companies like Home Depot and Pulte Homes. A less aggressive position would consist of IYR puts or puts on companies mentioned above. Another would be to buy S&P puts to equal the value of the house. If stocks crash 80 percent and we endure a 10-year depression, home values will likely drop 50 to 80 percent. That is a devastating blow for any home owner with a big mortgage. The hedge gains could do a lot to soften the blow from such a decline. With some guts and creativity, almost any asset or even business could find ways to ease the pain the crash will cause. Unfortunately, those who do this will stand out for their success. Others are

likely to blame them for the crash, when they should truly
be celebrated for their foresight and wisdom.

Let's now briefly consider an alternative investment—specifically,
the precious metal gold. It's a good idea to own some precious metal(s),
such as gold, in your portfolio going forward, because the coming
inflation will increase the price of gold and other precious metals. We
should also mention that gold is also highly emotional, and trying to
make money by timing the gold market requires a person to be either
(1) lucky or (2) an uncanny global mind reader. Don't try to time the
gold market; play it for the longer term.

Figure 12.4 illustrates the nominal price trend of gold from 1968
through year-end 2013. A logically good time to invest in gold was
during the inflationary period of the 1970s, when it became a popular hedge against inflation. Following the inflation blow off of the

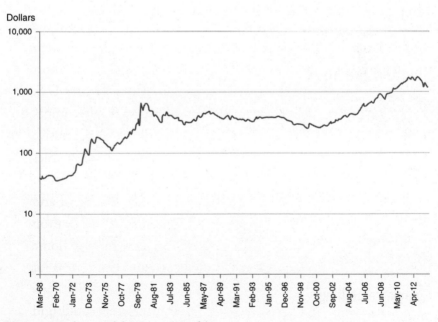

Figure 12.4   Gold Prices (Cash)
Source: Wall Street Journal.

early 1980s, investing in gold became an emotional business-cycle-the-world-is-coming-to-an-end kind of investment. It's noteworthy that gold experienced a tremendous asset price bubble beginning around 2003, compliments of the Federal Reserve's early forays into easing money into the economy. The large decline in gold prices that occurred through 2013 is likely leading us to a good long-term buying opportunity for gold and other precious metals—given the Federal Reserve and other central bankers' propensity toward loose monetary policy in an attempt to avoid short-term pain in the economy.

The takeaway from Figure 12.4 is that the next long-term buying opportunity will be directly related to when people begin to realize that future inflation *is indeed coming*. Once that perception takes hold, gold prices will rise significantly—until the inflation winds turn to *deflation* because of the Great Depression. Odds are that we won't have this broad-based perspective until we are on the other side of the 2014–2015 period of business cycle decline. But remember—it doesn't pay to try to time this market unless you are feeling particularly lucky or clairvoyant.

How Old Are You?

We are going to examine some investing guidelines that are roughly age specific. We say *roughly* because risk tolerances vary greatly and not always by age. You may be a very wealthy twenty-something, be financially limping toward retirement, or be anything in between. There are no *carte blanche* solutions or templates. Read the suggestions for each age category, and see if any might apply to you in your particular circumstances—or perhaps situations in which your children or parents might find themselves.

Twenty-Something

Assuming you are a typical twenty-something, you are probably just beginning your career and have not yet accumulated a lot of assets.

Your income is likely to go up as you gain responsibilities and additional skills in the future, but for now it feels like there isn't much left after meeting life's necessities and having had a little fun. Invest with the future in mind? You are too busy paying the rent and school loans, saving for the down payment on the car you want, saving for the house or condominium you want to buy, or saving for your next big vacation. What follows is what separates a lot of future-haves from almost-haves from have-nots.

You need to start saving and investing in your twenties. And you want to put away enough to have at least three months' living expenses on hand in case you lose your job. (Go ahead and assume you can move back in with your folks if you have been nice to them.) Amassing such a stockpile will require real discipline. You will have to forego spending on consumption today so that you can consume in the future. Don't feel bad if you cannot make yourself do this; neither can the U.S. federal government. But it will benefit you greatly if you can at least try.

If you have self-discipline and manage to create a nest egg, start putting money aside to invest—specifically, into asset categories that will appreciate in value (i.e., not that expensive car). Remember: you are young and can afford to take risks because time is on your side. Perhaps that means you want to favor mid-cap or small-cap stocks; you can ask your financial advisor which ETFs or mutual funds he or she prefers if you don't have your own opinion. You'll probably want to overweight stocks at the expense of bonds. At this age, it is likely that equities (stocks) will form the overwhelming majority of your portfolio. Although not consistent with traditional recommendations but probably realistic given what life is like, try to keep the equity allocation to no more than 70 percent of your portfolio, with the other 30 percent comprising cash, alternative investments, and maybe a pinch of fixed income.

The best time to take a loss is early in your investing career. It's easier to recover from losing money in your twenties than it is from losing that same percentage of money in your forties or beyond. Being in one's twenties carries with it the perception of powerful knowledge and insights into the world. Exercise those insights and that knowledge to do your best to try to beat the market. Perhaps you will find out you are indeed just that good. Perhaps you will find that you are indeed lucky. Perhaps you will find (before too long) that you should start playing it more conventionally and using math and time to make your fortune.

One more thing while you are still in your twenties: *pay cash*. Get loans for cars, homes, and other very large capital outlays. Necessities, such as eye exams and corrective lenses, can go on your credit card if you need them. But if you don't have the cash to buy that shirt, dress, bracelet, or watch or to see that movie—don't buy it until you have the cash. Using a credit card like a private printing press for money will leave you in a financial hole that will be extremely difficult to emerge from—and will almost always leave you wondering why so-and-so is so much better off financially when you pass through the twenties and enter into the next two decades. You already knew that, of course, but we had to be responsible and remind you anyway.

Thirty-Something

Congratulations! You aren't a kid anymore. You may even have kids of your own some time during this decade of your life. You haven't even come close to your peak earning years, but some sort of career path should be taking shape by now. The good habits and the disciplines you instilled in yourself in your twenties are no less valuable today. Now it's time for you to get more serious about proper asset allocation, diversification, understanding the miracle of compound interest—and realizing that you have 30 or more years to go before you retire, so you need consistently good returns versus that one grand thing that will set you up for life.

Remember when we talked about having a core portfolio earlier in this chapter—and how you would have *satellite investments* after establishing that core? Your thirties are the time to establish this core. Think of your portfolio as you would a human body: without core muscle strength, you will be prone to backaches, headaches, perhaps knee problems, and a host of other ailments. So get the core right in your thirties. If you aren't sure what this means for you, you could call upon our own money expert and guide, Clark Bellin[1] of Lincoln, Nebraska, if you want a one-to-one personal approach, or read Craig Israelsen's book *7Twelve* if you are more of a do-it-yourselfer.

In addition to establishing your core portfolio, you may be able to start tinkering with your satellite portfolio positions—things such as additional holdings in real estate, precious metals, and particular technologies. However, you also need to figure out how you are going to pay for Junior's college or trade school if you are going to go that route and haven't already funded the effort.

Despite lingering student loans and possible scary demographic projections pertaining to China and Europe, be sure that a big chunk of your portfolio is in real estate for the inflation hedge and the U.S. demographic play. Buy property with a view near or on water and in urban versus suburban areas. Let the laws of supply and demand work for you. Be sure to have at least 5 percent of your total wealth in inflation-protected investments if we have entered the new age of inflation. Real estate falls into this category, as do Treasury Inflation-Protected Securities (TIPS) and precious metals (long haul). Although suffering from some illiquidity in the secondary market, TIPS are an excellent vehicle to help pay for your daughter's or son's higher education.

Because the roaring twenties of your youth are behind you, it is time for you to conduct a yearly review of your portfolio and overall financial picture. Listening to the advice of Israelsen, rebalancing a core portfolio annually is often enough—but you cannot forget to do it.

---

[1] Clark offers securities and investment advisory services through NFP Securities, Inc., a member of the Financial Industry Regulatory Authority/Securities Investor Protection Corporation.

Cruising through your thirties means you need to temper some of the exuberance of youth, so you should probably ratchet down your equity exposure to 55 percent to 65 percent of your portfolio. Start buying some long-term bonds to comprise about 30 percent of your portfolio, and invest the balance in alternative investments. Ask yourself if you have sufficient life insurance, and consider additional questions regarding what kind of life insurance you should have. Though this is a topic for another book, you want to talk to someone you trust and figure out *why* you want the life insurance. Knowing why will usually allow you to determine how much.

Divert money into the future at every opportunity during your thirties by taking some of your increased wages, inheritance, lottery winnings, or whatever and putting—ideally—10 percent of your income into appreciating investments.

Forties and Fifties

These are usually your peak income years. You are shoveling money like crazy into your core portfolio and existing satellites or perhaps creating new satellites. Time and knowledge don't stand still and neither should your portfolio. But make sure you are still properly allocated among the asset classes to maximize long-term growth. At the same time, you need to start blending in more fixed-income investments. There is a very real temptation in this stage to overweight the winners and underweight those investment choices that haven't panned out as well—either within your portfolio or in the marketplace. Although a rebalancing of your portfolio is warranted, be ever mindful that time has a way of turning last year's financial winners into next year's losers.

Even though inflation will be tough on bonds, you are old enough now to be buying bonds with the thought of *holding them until maturity*. As we saw in Figure 12.2, you may find an opportune time to sell your bond just when you need to raise money, but you can't count on it during periods of prolonged inflation. Serendipity is not a working strategy. Calculate the *yield to maturity*—rather than current yield or coupon rate—on the bonds, because you are planning to hold them until they mature. Consider it a big win if you find the yield to maturity on the bond(s) attractive. *Attractive* is a relative term—but getting anything over 6 percent in this asset category would be a definite win in our book. Increasing the bond exposure within your portfolio takes some of the volatility out of the swings in how much you are worth. Remember, during a period of inflation, actual bonds, not bond funds, will provide you with more long-term safety from inflation risk.

You'll want to keep real estate and precious metals important parts of your core portfolio if the world is seven or more years away from 2030. You can generally start leavening in some caution with an eye toward fixed income as the fifties roll by and the sixties draw near. As you progress through this phase, a good guideline in our opinion is to work toward having 40 percent to 50 percent of your portfolio in bonds or some other fixed-income security before you round the bend on your fifties. Assuming the alternative portion is still present in the portfolio, you'll likely have around 30 percent to 40 percent in equities by the time you are done with your fifties.

Home Stretch toward Retirement

The final years leading up to actually retiring must be focused on wealth preservation versus accumulation. You do not want to put your capital at risk, because you can ill afford to see a drop in valuation this late in the game. Remember, a 10 percent decline in value requires a 20 percent rebound in prices—and 20 percent takes *time*, which you may not have that much of.

There aren't any real guarantees in the financial community. Everything can turn to mush under sufficiently adverse circumstances, particularly as current debt obligations in the United States and abroad impede the government's ability to deal with future crisis.

Understanding that, seek safety over appreciation. You will be flexing your portfolio more and more toward a future income stream—which likely means you'll leave the world of non-dividend-paying common stock increasingly behind you.

As a footnote: my friend Craig Israelsen points out in his book that mutual funds that are time targeted to your retirement generally don't work. You are going to have to make these decisions in concert with someone who is knowledgeable regarding your particular circumstances, income needs, and risk tolerances. Sorry—but there doesn't appear to be any easy one-size-fits-all plan based solely on age. When I (Brian) reach my mid-60s, I will likely have only satellite investments in common stock capital-appreciation plays, and the core portfolio will likely be locked down in income-producing, wealth-preservation-type assets.

Onset of the Great Depression: Good Advice for All Ages

There won't be billboards and proclamations from the government or otherwise when the coming Great Depression is about to begin—or when it eventually hits. There's no way to exactly time what's going to happen. Our recommendation is simply (1) don't get greedy, and (2) make sure you can sleep well at night the closer we get to 2030. When you think it is the right time—and we plan to be around via ITR Economics to help you with this—the plan is simple: *sell*. Stocks, bonds, real estate—sell it all. You don't want to own the assets that are dropping in value during the coming depression. You might want to hold on to your home, because you (and possibly your kids!) still need a place to live, but from a purely economic standpoint, the capital you could pull out of your home by selling it at a predepression high would pay for a lot of rent. At the very least, you may consider seriously downsizing at this time (again, assuming your kids don't need to come and live with you).

You have sold off these investments and are sitting on a boatload of cash. You might be holding U.S. dollars, yen, yuan, euros, or lire;

the list goes on. It really doesn't matter because our advice is the same no matter what you have: seek *safety!* That most likely means putting the money into some sort of secure annuity or purchasing government bonds. We expect the United States to be at the epicenter of the Great Depression—so *do not* buy U.S. government bonds. The timing is still far away (it is 2014 as we write this book), but current trends point to countries such as Canada, Australia, and Switzerland for safe governments. Our criteria include a combination of government indebtedness, availability of natural resources, demographics, and political stability.

If your timing is good (doesn't need to be great), you will be buying bonds near an interest rate high—because interest rates were consistently rising thanks to inflation. You will lock in a high rate of return via the current yield on these bonds and get a good yield to maturity should you decide to hold on to these bonds until they mature. Of course, you may not have this option if the bonds are issued as *callable* bonds. This means the issuing government can force you to sell the bond back to it (at a profit to you, if you do this right) when interest rates are once again low (or lower) and the government is trying to lower its interest expense. When the bonds are called—or about three to five years into the Great Depression—start easing back into buying hard assets. There's no need to rush, but you will want to establish this as a personal trend.

The key at the top of the Great Depression is to convert your investments from assets that appreciate into assets that *provide income*. This will require you to temporarily suspend anything similar to traditional asset allocation and engage in overweighting toward income-producing assets that aren't tied to asset prices the way that stocks and real estate are tied to the market. The government bonds approach cited earlier may not be right for you; you may want to consider fixed or variable annuities. Basically, you put in a lump of cash and make withdrawals from that lump plus any investment income that it earns for you. Not all annuities are the same, and we strongly advise consulting a certified financial planner with experience in this arena. The correct annuities and the government bonds will provide you with a conservative investment platform providing you with cash to live on and protection from asset prices falling.

In the next chapter we look at some possible road signs that will let us know when we are at the precipice of the Great Depression and it is time to overweight toward safety.

13 How to Spot the Top (Before the Great Depression)

Throughout most of this book, we have referred to the 2030–2040 Great Depression. Our unique business cycle theories indicate that this is the time frame we should have in mind. But economics is not an exact science; it could come a little sooner or conceivably a little later. We're more apt to believe "sooner" is more probable given when the entitlement program funding in the United States will become critical. Of course, there's always a chance that some exciting new technology or radical change in thinking at the governmental level will occur to forestall and perhaps even mitigate the downturn we envision. Although we might hope for such an occurrence, we cannot ignore reality.

Therefore, this chapter introduces eight road signs to depression that will apply whether the downturn starts in 2027 or 2033. It pays to remember that the sort of cycle we have discussed requires a *confluence* of events and trends. Avoid yelling that the end is near if any singular road sign appears. The U.S. and global economy are resilient enough that the downturn will truly require a combination of factors.

Dating from mid-2014, it is likely that we will experience three or four normal business cycles before the Great Depression occurs. At least two of these cycles will involve recession, and one or two could be soft landings—that is, what occurs when the economy *slows* down but doesn't *break* down. During a recession, the economy actively contracts, traditionally for two or more quarters. Think of the recessions between now and the coming Great Depression as corrective occurrences that adjust for some of the imbalances within the economic system on our way to the final top before the major decline.

Based on the past 22 recessions, as measured by the annual average index for U.S. industrial production, a normal recession involved a decline that lasted for 12 to 18 months. The peak-to-trough decline can be as mild as −3.6 percent or as severe as −19.5 percent. The recession of 2008–2009 was abnormally long at 21 months and certainly severe by modern standards at −14.6 percent. By contrast, a relatively recent but also severe recession occurred from 1980 to 1983. This lasted 31 months and encompassed a decline of 7.3 percent, but U.S. industrial production was back to record highs by 1984. It took considerably longer following the 2008–2009 downturn; it wasn't until late 2013 before the index reestablished record highs. Four years for a completed recovery and a resumption of growth is a long time. However, we expect that the decade following 2030 will be more like a more protracted period of stagnation—with incomplete recoveries followed by another recession, followed by an incomplete recovery, resulting in a decade with essentially zero—or only minimal—average per annum growth.

We are not expecting a repeat of the 1930s Great Depression in that the economy's volatility in that period was much greater than it is today and is likely to be in the future. During the last Great Depression, U.S. industrial production contracted 48.1 percent over 40 months and unemployment claimed 25 percent of the labor force. It's probable that the initial downward thrust in the coming Great Depression will be longer than 18 months (the longest normal length of decline) and more severe than both the −7.3 percent setback in the early 1980s and the 14.6 percent contraction that occurred from 2008 to 2009. That is the *initial thrust*. There will be a subsequent—albeit incomplete—recovery, and then another downward cycle, followed by another incomplete recovery until a decade has gone by and we have experienced a decade of essentially net zero growth. So if we experience a decline that hasn't lasted longer than 18 months or been more severe than 6.7 to 10.2 percent—and the recovery yields renewed record high levels of activity within 36 to 48 months of the initial trough—we didn't just endure the Great Depression. We simply underwent one of the warm-up cyclical recessions on our way to the Great Depression.

Leading indicators will decline as a prelude to the depression, but because they will have declined for prior business cycles, too, we can't count on these to help us tell the difference. The tricky part in foretelling that the coming cycle is the big one will be based on the *severity* of decline in a *system* of leading indicators—and determining which *particular indicators* are in fact heading downward in a hurry.

Eight Road Signs to Depression

1. The coming Great Depression is probably on our doorstep if people reach consensus that *inflation will stretch far into the future and commodity prices are projected to go higher*, and higher … and higher. During the 1970s, smart people were talking about oil prices that would be $200 a barrel and more. Although these extreme prices never materialized (fortunately!), people felt they were a strong possibility. When you see and hear that the people around you are convinced that gold, oil, or metals in general, or fuel sources in particular are going to go higher and higher—and when those people start to *plan on* those prices becoming reality—then you know you are getting closer to the day when the economic system will correct via a metaphorical reset button that results in a depression. We saw similar situations develop with the price of dot-com business

projections in the late 1990s and housing prices in 2005–2006.
People were sure prices would keep rising and they'd continue making fortunes—and we all saw how that ended. Unfortunately, we
don't seem to do very well at learning from history and experience.
This psychology will repeat itself before the projected depression.

2. Another signal may be *a three- to seven-year period of relative calm
before* the storm. Although the economy will likely be hit with a
recession around 2019, the period following that downturn should
lead to some reasonable prosperity. This relatively stable golden
age in the United States—based on our improving energy position
(including both self-reliance and exports)—could end up providing support for the U.S. dollar. This in turn would serve to keep
the worst aspect and most dismal numbers associated with inflation
at bay as we endure the first three to five years of the next decade.
The United States' good fortune through this period will enable the
country to temporarily ignore the increasingly destabilizing effects
brought about by the aging population, growing health care costs,
rising general inflation, higher interest rates, and the government
digging deeper into the private sector's pockets. Beware when people are convinced that peace and prosperity are upon us, and you
start reading headlines about the demise of the business cycle. It is
amazing how such pronouncements usually presage a downturn in
the economy.

3. Another road sign will be that *the older generation will be slow to
pass the mantle of power to generation X*, resulting in *increased levels of partisan rancor*. Failing to pass the mantle is a sign that we
won't have much luck developing a consensus on how to deal with
the depression drivers discussed in this book. It is a rare individual
who acknowledges that with age comes wisdom—and that wisdom may include that others' alternatives, workable views, or plans
are superior to our own. Normally, a person's thinking becomes
increasingly rigid after a certain age, and an aging population therefore enhances the probability of rigidly held partisan ideologies.

We seem to lose either our capability or our desire for discovering new ideas and perspectives. Historically, we overcame this problem by passing the mantle of power to the next (younger) generation. However, the fact that we are living longer has slowed this process down and diminished the political ability to implement real solutions in a timely manner. There is always hope of agreeable, middle-of-the-road solutions—but these do not appear to be the likely state of things as we look into the future.

4. You should worry about a pending depression if you see *business profits driven higher by increasing prices instead of increasing productivity.* There is evidence that the productivity improvement trend that characterized the past 20 to 30 years is waning. The need to seek out innovations and new competitive advantages is very real for the long-term solvency of our businesses as we approach the coming Great Depression. However, history suggests that the easier road to profits—that most widely traveled—will be to *raise prices faster* than the cost of the factors of production (applicable to service companies and manufacturers). Higher profits lead to higher stock valuations or improved lifestyles for the owners of capital. This easier road will ultimately leave us unprepared for the harsh reality of economic competition during the Great Depression. If you notice profits being increasingly driven by pricing prowess instead of advances in engineering or process improvement, be concerned that the economy is losing its ability to compensate for imbalances building within it. You can be fairly sure that the reset button of the Great Depression is that much closer.

5. Look for relatively *extreme imbalances within the economic system* (e.g., within the United States, within China, and within other large economies) *as opposed to imbalances between economies.* We are likely to experience relative prosperity within the global economic system until the level of inflation reaches near double-digit levels in the world's developed economies. Prosperity means less intercountry rancor and a decreased likelihood of trade barriers escalating

into trade wars. The renewed trend toward bilateral trade agreements may gain more traction, which would benefit country-to-country relationships. The road sign of imbalances *within* an economic system includes economic class warfare—whether real or driven by manipulated data—inflation causing strife within the society, and education becoming too expensive without more government intervention. Watch for evidence of these types of imbalances to signal trouble.

6. Be careful when you hear *pundits and leaders alike espousing that "This time it will be different"*—that is, not as bad as previous economic downturns—in the face of history and logic. It is not uncommon that a business we are working with can see—based on leading indicators and internal metrics—that the good times are about to end. Yet management believes that growth will continue because the past is irrelevant and that "It will be different *this time.*" The same thing will occur with the stock market at some point in the future: it will be climbing ever higher in a gravity-defying trend. Eventually, only a few will wonder or bother to question how or whether this growth is sustainable. There will be no logical answer for the unwarranted climb, but plenty of people will offer new theories of a dead business cycle or a new paradigm—which is just a variation on the statement that "It will be different this time." Be very careful when you see this happening in the stock market and in relation to economic growth. We should not—truly, we cannot—ignore higher debt and all the assorted problems we have described, but people will ignore them and will talk about unfettered growth based on gossamer wings. Add this to your road signs; indeed it may be the last that will appear before the drop occurs.

7. There is likely to be a *changing of the guard in the future*. Parts of Africa, East Europe, and Central America will gain ground regarding economic relative importance, much as China, Brazil, India, and Russia were constant headline news in the prior period.

These newer headline economies will have the advantage of (1) younger populations, (2) vast natural resources to harvest, (3) a lack of rules geared to protect the economic status quo, or (4) some combination of the three. Notice that all three of these elements are simple restatements of the depression drivers (trends) that inform much of what we know about the future.

8. It is a near certainty that *politicians and Keynesian-minded economists will make assertions* during the next 15 years that the very fact that the country has *not* gone bankrupt—and that the world is still buying U.S. debt—is proof positive *that all is under control.* Though not scientific or even especially logical, their claims will provide many in the population with solace. It is a variation of the so-called logic about any bad habit: I know cigarette smoking is bad per se, but how bad can it be in my case because I can still breathe just fine?

In the next chapter we look at some specifics that the next generation needs to know to effectively manage lives and businesses through the coming changes, regardless of when the road signs cited in this chapter occur.

14 What the Next Generation Needs to Know

Six Things the Next Generation Must Do

It is true that there is nothing as constant as change, and our economic future will require a lot of adaptability on the part of the next generation of business owners, leaders, and managers. The economic landscape will provide challenges for which they have no experience and have received little, if any, education or training. This chapter provides tomorrow's leaders and investors with ideas and information they will need to succeed.

What Owners and Managers Must Do

The industrialized world has not seen systemic inflation since the early 1980s. That means an entire generation has grown up without feeling its effect or knowing how to manage through it. They cannot conceive of a consumer price index reaching 5 percent, 7 percent, and then 10 percent; as a result, they are not ready to lead their companies and employees through these inevitably tumultuous times.

They're also going to have to look at contracts differently. A number of price indexes can provide a useful metric for negotiating contract escalators. We covered this subject more extensively in Chapter 5. For now, we'll simply remind you that multiyear contracts that utilize the proper producer or materials price index will make the difference between profitability and losing money.

You also need to manage inventory differently during periods of inflation. A just-in-time approach may not be in your best interest as inflation heats up. Businesses may also benefit from borrowing and making major purchases in the early stages of a longer-term inflationary cycle, because preinflation purchases provide for lower-cost expenditures. Financing those expenditures means you will be using inflated, easier-to-get dollars to repay the fixed costs. That strategy can return huge dividends as you increase your company's market position while gaining a financial advantage.

The overarching need for business leaders in the years between now and 2030 will be to manage the escalating cost structure while also managing the workforce's expectations. This will require you to realize that you must quickly adapt to the new things happening around you and changed economic landscape. The old way will not work—and slow adapters may not get a second chance.

Inflation *breeds inefficiency*. Price increases become relatively easy to pass along, and companies can use this to mask problems in internal processes or in particular systems. Winning owners and managers will not follow the easy path of price increases but will relentlessly push efficiency gains while raising prices. This will improve cash flow and the bottom line, both of which will be essential to surviving the coming Great Depression or in positioning the company for a high-multiple sale to new owners in the coming decade. Competitors who rely on inflation as their profit strategy will be hard-pressed to survive the coming depression. Any slowdown in activity will go straight to their bottom line, but the efficient firm can maintain per-unit profitability.

There was a time when an engineer, scientist, programmer, or other technically brilliant person could start and lead a firm for years before worrying about the complexities of managing people and the higher goal of leadership. The demographic trends we've addressed in this book suggest that it will be harder to find talented team members with technical *and* interpersonal skills as we approach 2030. A tightening labor market means that potential employees will have greater pick over where they want to work and whom they want to follow. Today's young leaders with technical backgrounds should pursue a master of business administration program or something similar and work diligently on their leadership skills now. This will position them to attract the best and the brightest workforce available and to build a cohesive high-profit team. On-the-job training in this area will be too slow and too expensive in terms of lost opportunities.

The preceding paragraphs require a willingness to change methods and to adapt to extant conditions—a personality trait that will become invaluable when the depression begins. Leaders will need to adjust to the downturn quickly. They must discuss, outline, and revise plans for dramatically lower levels of activity as we get closer to 2030. Human nature will cause too many people to hope that the problems are only temporary and that the storm will quickly pass. It won't. Business leaders will need to implement well-thought-out plans quickly if the business and a large section of the workforce are going to successfully make it through the downturn. This will require plans for managing dramatically lower levels of cash in a harsh environment.

The six pieces of advice we give our kids today are applicable to businesses and make for a solid outline for businesses that wish to survive the 2030s.

Six Things Our Kids (and Businesses) Must Do

We all want our children to not only survive but also thrive during the coming Great Depression. Earlier chapters have provided investment ideas they should undertake between now and 2030. The following are six simple steps that will ensure they fare well when the world around them seems to be falling apart.

1. *Younger people must learn to live below their means and invest in their own future*, and they must do this from an early age. Nearly everyone should save some money from each paycheck and use these savings to invest in *equities* as the 2020s should provide a better-than-inflation return on investment. The goal is to maximize the nest egg so that people who are poised to retire or who lose their jobs won't be destitute and depend on a government that has lost the wherewithal to provide generous entitlements.

2. *Learning a second language* in addition to English is advisable further along in the more formal education process. English is a near-universal business language. In addition to English, French will be a sought-after language. French, like English, is widely known, and it is a useful fallback language in many parts of Africa. Africa holds great promise for the future, and being able to communicate in either English or French is going to be a real competitive advantage.

3. *Each household, even households of one, should have multiple income streams*. This way, when one source of cash comes under pressure or fails, the other will be there to help maintain the household. Dividends and rental property make excellent sources of additional income that can be saved for future use. Two wage earners in the same household should be careful that they are not working in the same industry or in the same section of the business cycle. For instance, having both earners in the machinery export business all but guarantees both incomes will be negatively affected at the same time. Two teachers in the same school system might face simultaneous cutbacks and layoffs. Households need to diversify when possible; for example, one in business and the other in law enforcement, in the fire department, in the medical field, in the insurance industry, in teaching, or in caring for senior citizens. Two incomes

in business or in the same field will dramatically increase the risk of financial troubles.

4. *Have an income that one of the Great Depression drivers stimulates specifically.* The two drivers to focus on in this context are *demographics* and *inflation*. A field of study and career in the pursuit of making life better, healthier, longer, or with an improved lifestyle is certainly going to be great business with the world's population growing by a billion people between now and the middle of this century. But also in this category of demographic opportunity is the field of *entertainment*. As the middle class on planet Earth expands, leisure time in search of entertainment is likely to be a burgeoning and potentially lucrative field. In the inflation arena, natural resources warrant a primary focus for students and professionals. Harvesting and conserving natural resources are going to be very important and ultimately complementary endeavors in an age when the intrinsic value of natural resources is climbing.

5. *Our kids must pay off their entire debt load, or at least as much as possible, by 2030.* The minimum they must do is pay off the mortgage and any car loans by 2030. Credit card collectors can be nasty, but they cannot take your home. Student loans should be paid off if possible, but failure here will also not bring about homelessness. Of course, the best advice is to have *everything* paid off—this provides for the highest amount of available cash in the event of dramatic income reduction. No one can repossess what you own outright. Protect your future by planning how you will be debt free by 2030.

6. *Be ready to buy.* Doing the preceding three things will provide the opportunity for great wealth creation. The stock market will crash in the depression, which means equity prices on great companies will be cheap. People with cash can move in and create future fortunes by being ready to buy. Those who will use the depression to their advantage will also be ready to buy real estate, as those values and their rental incomes will surely escalate in a post-depression economy.

Last, be ready to buy businesses in their entirety because the aging demographic and the sour economy will produce incredible deals on entities that will eventually once again be sound cash-producing businesses. Look for competitors who are running out of hope and cash—or seek out these attributes in entirely new fields—and you will find that you have created the basis for a business empire that may make you and your offspring very wealthy in the 2040s and beyond.

Most people will fear the coming Great Depression and will hope only to survive. The steps outlined here for our kids, as well as our businesses, will turn the worst economic downturn in a century into the opportunity of a lifetime. The preparation needs to begin now.

15 Is There Hope?

One of the great things about people is their ability to look forward to the future. Granted, the tomorrow we've described in this book appears quite disturbing. Who wants a Great Depression to affect most of the world? However, the facts point toward a certain reality—and we have tried to present paths for individuals and companies that will lead to a *better* future, one that will help them not just survive but also succeed.

People often ask us if anything would or could change our view of the future and make the path and strategies presented here irrelevant. There are indeed some game-changing events that we describe next that could provide for a different future than the likely scenario discussed throughout the book. But, even if there is a future without a Great Depression, the strategies and actions we have described will help you establish and maintain a sense of financial security.

What Can Stave Off the Great Depression of 2030?

Government and policy makers can make a huge difference in our future by setting aside politically driven, uncompromising ideology and seeking compromise on vexing issues. Congress and the executive branch have the power to reshape the future by aggressively *pushing out the retirement age* for the millennial generation (born 1977–1994) and generations that follow. Increasing the years of contribution into the health care and Social Security systems would have a dramatic impact on solvency. Today's 40-year-olds would have to agree (in the voting booth) that they will work until they are 72; 30-year-olds, to 75; and so on. Many of them will have to out of economic necessity, and thus, the legal change may not be as draconian as it first appears. There will be a demand for their talents in the workplace given baby boomers' retirement and a need for them to pay taxes longer than boomers had to. At present, there is not any large-scale movement in Congress or in the population for these changes to occur—and the longer we wait, the more dramatic the changes must be.

Government at all levels could also decide that *austerity* is the road to stability and then to prosperity. Our leaders would have to decide to live within their means and to fund only mission critical programs—a concept that runs entirely contrary to the current two-year House of Representatives election cycle and to the way Congress operates. This new path would require a repudiation of special interest groups and a change in philosophy that would require Congress to focus more on national than state interest. Congress members are, of course, elected to represent the people of their state, and not the national population; therefore, a dramatic change in congressional focus and a development of a mission-critical format are not likely.

Our culture could also decide to dedicate itself to physical fitness, nutritious eating, and healthy lifestyles—something that would dramatically reduce health care costs for more than just the baby boomers. This alone could save untold billions of dollars and significantly affect our future. However, our current system provides no financial incentive for individuals to make the necessary changes in their lives. A change to a demonstrably healthier population, especially among senior citizens, seems about as likely as a comet hitting the planet (another event that would drastically alter the future and our projections about a depression!).

Technological advances could significantly affect our future for the better. A new energy source has the power to boost the U.S. economy and tax revenues substantially, much as the computer age and the Internet did. However, it is critical that the technology say "made in the United States" on the box if the revenues, jobs, and taxes are going to accrue to the nation with the biggest problem.

A new medical technology would have the greatest impact on the future; imagine, for example, advances that would eliminate the need for new knees and hip replacements. Medical breakthroughs such as these could allow us to treat conditions, including macular degeneration, arthritis, pulmonary problems, and similar ailments, cheaply and easily. It sounds unbelievable, but it could happen. Biotech companies in different parts of the world—such as Bio-Time in San Francisco—are working to make *regenerative medicine* available to all of us. This approach consists of engineering tissues and therapy from stem cells derived from the patient's own body. Although this amazing science is in its infancy, it has promise—and *could* become commonplace over the next 10 to 20 years. Unfortunately that may be too late to make a difference.

Any new technology is going to take a serious amount of time to develop; it must undergo trials and human testing and will then finally make it to the market here in the United States. It is not likely that anything will arrive in time, although we certainly like the thought. A cure for cancer or any number of other illnesses would be fantastic from a social standing—but would not necessarily help with health care costs if the treatment is expensive.

We have already discussed how other major nations—those with deep pockets that might at one time have loaned us the money to meet our ever-increasing obligations—will be experiencing their own problems. Their homegrown problems will be serious enough to keep them focused on internal issues versus risking more money on a debt-laden United States.

A Different View of the 1930s

Every movie, picture, or media portrayal of the 1930s Great Depression depicts severe hardship: long lines of hungry people, homes being foreclosed upon, and massive unemployment. We once asked our mother about her childhood in the Great Depression. Much to our surprise, she told us that she did not even realize there was a Great Depression until later. She told us that her father, our grandfather, was a conservative man who planned well. He did not lose his job, and he had no massive change in fortune because of the stock market crash or home value declines. He continued to provide for his family. Mom even said that they ate like they always ate and lived as they had always lived—simply.

This is the goal we should each have as we prepare for the 2030s. We will strive to protect our children and grandchildren from harm and deprivation so that they can tell their *children* that they did not suffer. Indeed, they can do much more by following the precepts in this book; they can create lasting wealth.

A Different Future

The 2030s will provide many of us with an unparalleled opportunity to show others that business leaders and investors are also philanthropists. There will be no lack of opportunities to help your fellow human—whether it's through job fairs, food pantries, and short-term work opportunities, among others. It will also be a time when we can do the most good for our workforce by *being prepared*. This preparedness will provide employment for millions in America—which means that millions of households will make it through the depression without hunger or loss.

It is our hope that the kindness and largesse of business in the 2030s will show two generations that corporate leaders are not evil or greedy.

We hope that the false promises of a free-spending government will be exposed, and people will see the value of hard work, planning, education, and entrepreneurship. The cold realities of the 2030s might just awaken that spirit of self-reliance that provides for jobs, innovation, the arts, medical advances, and comfort in retirement.

Summary

We are entrepreneurs, which means we are among the most hopeful people you will ever want to meet. Entrepreneurs make a dream reality by taking risks and working hard. If a person did not believe in that dream—if a person did not really believe that it would become as he or she had envisioned—then there would be no hope. No one would ever take those first steps. We are brothers who hope for a better tomorrow for our families, our many friends and clients, and our team members. If we did not, we would pack it in today.

Having said that, we have to take a realistic view of the future and properly assess the risks as we take our families and our company into the future. Yes, technology or brotherly love could change the future—and we might never have the Great Depression of 2030. Government could reach tremendous compromises that change the United States into a once-again fiscally solvent economic force. There *is* that possibility. However, a cold look at reality says it is not worth the risk of ignoring all the trends and statistics to hope blindly that the future will be different. All of us must act as good stewards of that which we have and make preparations for the coming storm. A sea captain would be a fool to ignore the weather reports and sail blindly forth without proper gear or preparation. A worthy captain prepares his or her ship and crew for what is coming so that they may successfully navigate the waters and safely reach their destination. Sail on and fare thee well!

BIBLIOGRAPHY

Associated Press. "Bernanke: Fed Ready to Cut Interest Rates Again: 'We Stand Ready to Take Substantive Additional Action,' Fed Chief Says." NBCNews.com (January 10, 2008). www.nbcnews.com/id/22592939.

Bernanke, Ben S. "The Subprime Mortgage Market." Speech given at the Federal Reserve Bank of Chicago's 43rd Annual Conference on Bank Structure and Competition, Chicago, May 17, 2007.

Center on Budget and Policy Priorities. "Policy Basics: Where Do Our Federal Tax Dollars Go?" Last modified April 12, 2013. www.cbpp.org/cms/index.cfm?fa=view&id=1258.

Congressional Budget Office. *The 2013 Long-Term Budget Outlook*. Last modified October 31, 2013. https://cbo.gov/publication/44521.

Desjardins, Lisa. "Why the U.S. May Never Have a Balanced Budget Again." CNN.com (March 29, 2012). www.cnn.com/2012/03/29/politics/balanced-budget.

Ehrlich, Paul R. *The Population Bomb*. San Francisco: Sierra Club/Ballantine Books, 1970.

Federal Reserve Bank of St. Louis. "State and Local Governments, Excluding Employee Retirement Funds; Credit Market Instruments; Liability, Level (SLG-SDODNS)." 2013. http://research.stlouisfed.org/fred2/series/SLGSDODNS.

Greenlaw, David, James D. Hamilton, Peter Hooper, and Frederic S. Mishkin. "Crunch Time: Fiscal Crises and the Role of Monetary Policy." Paper presented at the U.S. Monetary Policy Forum, New York City, February 22, 2013.

Israelsen, Craig L. *7Twelve: A Diversified Investment Portfolio with a Plan*. Hoboken, NJ: John Wiley & Sons, 2010.

KPMG International. "Corporate Tax Rates Table." Accessed March 8, 2014. www.kpmg.com/global/en/services/tax/tax-tools-and-resources/pages/corporate-tax-rates-table.aspx.

Meadows, Donella H., Dennis L. Meadows, Jørgen Randers, and William W. Behrens III. *The Limits to Growth*. New York: Signet, 1972.

Office of Management and Budget. "Table 1.3—Summary of Receipts, Outlays, and Surpluses or Deficits (–) in Current Dollars, Constant (FY 2005) Dollars, and as Percentages of GDP: 1940–2018." Accessed March 8, 2014. www.whitehouse .gov/omb/budget/Historicals.

Smith, Jaynie L. *Creating Competitive Advantage: Give Customers a Reason to Choose You over Your Competitors*. With William G. Flanagan. New York: Crown Business, 2006.

Social Security and Medicare Boards of Trustees. "A Summary of the 2013 Annual Reports." Social Security Administration. 2013. www.ssa.gov/OACT/TRSUM.

Torres, Craig, and Scott Lanman. "Bernanke Says Risk of 'Substantial Downturn' Has Diminished." Bloomberg (June 9, 2008). www.bloomberg.com/apps/ news?pid=newsarchive&sid=aH6u3wsqwMFM.

U.S. Census Bureau. "International Data Base." Last modified December 19, 2013. www.census.gov/population/international/data/idb/region.php?N=%20 Results%20&T=10&A=both&RT=0&Y=2030&R=120,130,142,150&C=# IDBTOP.

INDEX